MY ROMANCE WITH FOOD

ROOPA NABAR

Popular Prakashan
www.popularprakashan.com

Published by
Harsha Bhatkal
for Popular Prakashan Pvt. Ltd.
301, Mahalaxmi Chambers
22, Bhulabhai Desai Road
Mumbai 400026
info@popularprakashan.com

First Published 2022

(4541)
ISBN 978-81-955127-1-3

Concept and Design - **Devaki Bavkar**

Food Styling - **Anupa Das**

Photography - **Nisha Dingra**

Content writer - **Sonica Sunderram**

Author's note photo - Nitin Sapkale

Cover location - courtesy Sanjeev Kapoor studio

Cover picture - Saree and blouse by Suta (Insta suta_bombay)

Printed in India
by Print Plus Private Limited
212, Swastik Chambers, ST Road, Chembur, Mumbai 400071

While this book is inspired by four amazingly beautiful and strong women in my life, I dedicate it to four equally strong and amazing men who are the pillars in the canopy of my life. My dad Shashikant Patki, my brother Dr Ameet Patki, my husband Dr Sanjay and my son Gaurang.

Thank you for always seeing the good in me even on the rare occasions when I couldn't see it myself!

Hi,

Those of you who know me personally know that I do have the gift of the gab and I love to talk as much as I love to cook and eat. In fact, so much so that the first words I ever uttered were 'hotel mum-mum'. Not mom- or dad or aaji, but hotel mum-mum. Now at 58, when I look back at my life and see the role food has played in it - it makes complete sense.

Growing up in Mumbai in the most loving joint family, my childhood was joyous and my teenage years were carefree! I studied to be a paramedic, started working at the age of 21 and got married to a handsome doctor when I was 22. By the time I hit 23 I had my son and was well settled in my job. While this sequence of events might sound mundane, my life was anything but that! This black and white outline is actually painted with a rainbow of colours of beautiful moments - vacations across the globe, candlelit dinners at home, my son's birthday parties and the annual torture of PTA meetings, delightful trips to my hometown, office gossip, doctors conferences, poojas, festivals and a lot more! In 2011, in between all this excitement, my professional food journey began as I participated in the FoodFood Maha Challenge and actively shared recipes on shows like Amhi Saare Khavaiye, Sanjeev Kapoor Khazana and India Food Network. That's when I knew my hobby had turned into a passion, the rest as they say is history!

So, while the shoots, pop-ups and food tastings kept me busy, the idea of writing a cookbook was always at the back of my mind. I knew it is what will help me preserve my love for food and the culinary memories with my loved ones for posterity and beyond digital footprints. When the Covid-Pandemic put the world on a standstill in the summer of 2020, the wheels on My Food Romance started moving - slowly but steadily.

This book is a culmination of all my food experiences. Anecdotes from aaji and aai, tips from travels and farmer market visits across the world, Chef's Kapoor's pearls of wisdom, knowledge from the internet and culinary books, plus my own intuition and years of permutations and combinations in the kitchen! Besides traditional Maharashtrian recipes, I also showcased the best of my kitchen experiments with recipes from other parts of the country and globe.

Through the process of compiling, testing and tasting the recipes, jotting down the anecdotes and smiling like a proud parent as my creations got clicked for the book - I revisited all my favourite sights, smells and sounds in my happy place, my kitchen!

Now I am giving you an all-access pass into my kitchen and I promise, as you try every recipe you too will feel the love, elation and absolute satisfaction that I have felt. I hope you feel the magic of local ingredients like alsandes and aluche phatphate, the spice hit in coconutty fish curries, the inciting aromas of a majestic dum biryani and of course the comfort in each morsel of varan-bhaat.

I hope you enjoy every page of 'My Romance with Food' as much as I enjoyed putting it together for you!

With Love,

Roopa Nabar

FOREWORD

Cooking great food requires respect for ingredients, understanding of cuisines and a passion and love to feed people - Roopa Nabar's cooking has all of that in abundance.

My first interaction with her was on the sets of Food Food Maha Challenge where one of the main criteria while selecting contestants on the show was a passion and a spark that we saw in them.

As I write the foreword for this book, I am sure we made the right decision with Roopa!

This book 'My Romance with Food' which documents traditional Maharashtrian, especially GSB cuisine, takes the journey of food in our country beyond the borders and demographics - giving you a taste of little known ingredients, techniques and wonderful flavours!

My Romance with Food, by Roopa Nabar is one such book - a great read for those who love food from the soul and stories from the heart!

BEVERAGES

SNACKS & STARTERS

VEGETABLES

CONTENTS

CONTENTS

Native Village Kitchen

For most of us, it is the flavours that we taste during our childhood that we end up chasing and craving later in life. That's why 'maa ke haath ka khaana', samosas from your school canteen and the little treats during summer holidays at your grandparents' home always remain our favourite food, no matter how far we travel and how much we eat. Well, I am no different and childhood trips to my native village have had a big impact on my culinary sensibilities and hence also in this book.

I still have a mental picture almost as fresh as the plethora of seafood that awaited us following the eight-hour bus and then a twenty minute-long wobbly bullock cart ride to our colossal house in Prabhanvalli, near Ratnagiri. Its large spacious rooms and mystical corridors, all connected to the gigantic kitchen in the centre.

I remember waking up to the smell of breakfast infused with the aroma of a wood fire. While on most days it would be simple rice porridge or bhaatachi pej and a spicy, tangy backyard vegetable preparation called dabdabit, the woody aroma from the clay chulah would be new every day. It took me many years to realise that the type of wood and clay added their own flavours and aromas to the food.

Some mornings, my siblings and I accompanied my uncle to the nearby river or seashore to fish. We returned with an assortment of prawns, sardines (pedvey), mackerels (bangda) and sometimes even a sackful of oysters – all to be cooked and relished for lunch on the very same day. Delicious good meals of flatbread (bhakri), stir-fry (fish sukka), fish curry (amti) or dal, rice, sol kadhi and a buffet of fried fish or rawa fried oysters – no portions sizes, no courses, no rules, just the pure joy of good food!

Besides fishing, even hunting for game was not uncommon back in the day. On such occasions when my uncle would leave with his shotgun, lunch would be bhakri, rice and spicy brown meat curry of rabbits, partridge or wild boars spiced with whole garam masala, onion, dry and fresh coconut.

My aaji also made puffed red rice laddoos flavoured with jaggery and cardamom – a tea-time treat made with the basic essentials at home.

It was the highlight of a pure vegetarian feast made by villagers during the yearly Devi cha Gondhal festivities in our village. Gondhal is a festival that is celebrated in honour of the community Goddess. It happens

during the wedding season in the village, which at the time coincided with our summer holidays. Digging into the pure vegetarian feast put out by all the villagers, watching the balya folk dance performed by balyagadis with fire torches in their hands and of course the collective festive atmosphere –Today, those are some of my most treasured memories.

Luckily for me, these hometown trips didn't end with my childhood. Soon after Sanjay and I got married, we visited his ancestral place, Shiroda in Maharashtra along the Goa border. It's a wonderful little seaside village surrounded by lush coconut palms, paddy fields and salt pans. Our yearly vacations here were divided between breezy days spent in the courtyard of our home in Shiroda and visiting family temples for poojas and aarti's in our Kuladeva temple of Lord Mangesh in Goa. Both these parts of the holiday include food in brilliant formats. If you ask me today, I would pick the pure vegetarian temple feasts over shack evenings of beer and chilli chicken on the beach, without a blink! The magic of a full course meal of varan-bhaat, chutneys, koshimbir (salads), sandge (papads), usal (black pea curries), bhaaji

(vegetable stir-fries), and a dessert of mangana (sweet porridge) is not something you can just create with a few clicks on an app. It is something that is a labour of love, a test of tradition and a taste of home, and that my friends, is what will really give you that feeling of nirvana – a smile on your face, satisfaction in your hearts and probably even a halo around your head!

KHANAWAL

'Pop-up Kitchens' might be a new word, but the concept is an old one, at least in the GSB community in the form of a 'Khanawal'. This kitty party of sorts comprises a full-course, sit-down traditional thali prepared by the lady hosting the Khanawal. The number of seats is limited and the menu is fixed. The thali has rice, fish curry and fried fish – depending upon the catch of the day. There is almost always a stir-fried preparation called 'Sukka' which can be made with clams (tisrya), crab (kurli) or oyster (kalwa) and a dry fish preparation called Kishmoor. The thali is not complete without roasted papad, a seasonal pickle and sol kadhi. Chapatis are given on request. And a food coma, like in the case of most home-cooked meals, is guaranteed.

KOKUM

After traveling across continents, meeting many people and eating many, many meals, I've come to realize that people and food have more in common than not. While our constitution is the same, each cuisine, like every person, has certain things that make them unique and stand out amongst each other. In Maharashtrian coastal cuisine Kokum is one of those ingredients.
A native to the Konkan coast, kokum in its raw form is known as 'Raatamba'. The fruit is super sour and used more as a souring agent than a fresh fruit. It is a blessing and a base for many recipes. Want to add a tang to curries? Use kokum! Want to add some vitamins and minerals to your diet - get some kokum! Want to beat coastal humidity with a cool summer drink - Kokum again! We are so obsessed with this fruit that we have found ways to preserve and store enough to last us the entire year. The preservation is done with the two most basic preservatives known to mankind - salt or sugar. Both create a different version of the kokum extract. The cavity of the raatamba fruit when filled with sugar and left out for a couple of days till the sugar de-crystallizes gives you a sweet, tangy, bright pink coloured syrup used to make Kokum Sherbet - the Konkan Coasts' favourite summer drink! The same raatamba fruit is also salted to create agal - a salted extract of this beautiful fruit which is used to make sol kadhi and a host of other preparations. Like every other rural custom - nothing goes to waste. After deriving this fantastic salty concentrate, these kokum petals are further sun dried to create aamsul, which adds flavour to our curries and stir fries all through the year. While we do also use souring agents like tamarind and vinegar in our cooking, during the course of this book, you will see that kokum has a special place in our kitchen, our palate and definitely in our hearts!

सोल

SOL KADHI

Coconut and Kokum Beverage

Sol kadhi is fondly called pink kadhi by the little ones in my family because of its baby pink colour. In a Saraswat household, the meal is incomplete without sol kadhi and rice or kadhi-bhaat at the end.

Ingredients:

2 cups grated fresh coconut

8-10 kokum petals (aamsul)

½ teaspoon asafoetida (hing)

Salt to taste

2 green chilies

4-5 garlic cloves

4-5 black peppercorns

1 tablespoon finely chopped fresh coriander leaves

Fresh coriander sprigs for garnish

Method:

Place the kokum in a large bowl, add the asafoetida, salt and half a cup of water. Set aside for five minutes.

Place the grated coconut, green chillies, garlic and black peppercorns into a grinder jar and grind to a coarse paste. Add one and a half cups of water and grind well.

Strain the ground mixture through a strainer or a muslin cloth into the kokum mixture. Add one cup water and adjust salt and mix well.

Add the chopped coriander and mix till well combined. Let the mixture rest for ten minutes. You can also discard the kokum petals and refrigerate till chilled.

Pour into individual serving glasses and garnish with coriander sprig. Serve chilled.

Preparation Time: 10-15 minutes
Cooking Time: 0 minutes
Serves: 4-5

PHUTI KADHI कढी

Fresh Kokum Fruit Beverage

Sweet and tangy with a hint of spice - the flavours in a phuti kadhi are magical and light. You can easily drink several glasses without a second thought. The recipe is easy and the taste, absolutely refreshing, while the colour is the colour of passion - a bright ruby red. If these reasons aren't enough to make you try it out, let me tell you that Phuti Kadhi is also a great digestive - perfect for all those rice dominant meals plans.

Ingredients:

4 - 5 fresh kokum fruits (Ratambe), cut into quarters

Salt to taste

1 teaspoon sugar

½ teaspoon ghee

½ teaspoon mustard seeds

1 green chilli, finely chopped

¼ teaspoon asafoetida (hing)

2 tablespoons finely chopped fresh coriander leaves

Method:

Place the fresh kokum quarters in a bowl, add three cups of water and set it aside to soak for one hour. Discard the fresh kokum quarters and add salt and sugar.

Heat the ghee in a pan, add the mustard seeds and let them splutter. Add the green chilli, asafoetida and add it to the kokum mixture and mix well.

Add the coriander leaves and serve.

Preparation Time: 1 hour
Cooking Time: 0-5 minutes
Serves: 4

If you do not have fresh kokum, you can use readymade kokum juice concentrate (salted). You will need half a cup of concentrate for this recipe.

NEER FANAS

KAAPA

कापं

Breadfruit Fritters

Neer Fanas tree in a Konkan backyard is as common as basil in an Italian one. Neer Fanas or bread-fruit belongs to the jackfruit family, but are rounder and much smaller in size. Once fried, the kaape resembles fried fish–in appearance, taste, and texture. So on days when we are vegetarian at home, neer phanas on the menu adds a meaty, umami taste to the meal.

Ingredients:

1 medium neer phanas (breadfruit), peeled

Salt to taste

¼ cup semolina

½ cup rice flour

1 teaspoon red chilli powder

½ teaspoon turmeric powder

1 teaspoon sambar powder *(pg no. 153)*

Oil for shallow-frying

Method:

Halve the neer phanas lengthwise and further cut each half into half- inch thick semi-circular pieces. Place them in a bowl. Add the salt and mix well.

Spread the semolina and rice flour on a plate. Add salt, red chilli powder, turmeric powder and sambar powder and mix well.

Heat oil in a non-stick shallow pan.

Coat each neer phanas piece with the semolina-rice flour mixture on both sides and gently slide in a few pieces into the hot oil. Cover for two minutes, flip the pieces and cook till golden brown and cook on both sides (Approx. six to eight minutes on medium heat). Drain on absorbent paper.

Arrange the pieces on a serving plate and serve.

Preparation Time: 5-10 minutes
Cooking Time: 10-15 minutes
Serves: 4-5

KISHMOOR

Dry Shrimps Salad

The name definitely has a romantic ring, doesn't it? Well, for the locals in this part of the world (and my husband), this dry fish salad or Kishmoor is quite the epitome of romance. While the world associates 'rains with romance', for us GSB's (Gaud Saraswat Brahmins) it is 'rains and kishmoor'. It is what adds a spark to our meals during the monsoon when fresh fish is not easily available. These tiny, dried shrimps with all that concentrated salty flavour come to their full glory when mixed with fresh coconut and tangy tamarind. I always end up eating a much larger portion than is normally accepted for an accompaniment and I'm sure with this recipe you will too!

Heat **1 tablespoon coconut oil** in a non-stick pan. Add **1 cup dried shrimps, head and tail removed** and roast lightly till crisp. Remove from heat and set aside. Combine **1 medium, finely chopped onion, salt, a pinch of turmeric powder, ½ teaspoon red chilli powder** and **1 teaspoon tamarind pulp** in a bowl and mix well. Add **¼ cup fresh scraped coconut** and mix well. Add fried shrimps and mix again. Serve immediately.

It is important to remove the heads and tails of the dried shrimps as they are quite sharp to eat. However, nowadays, you do get pre cleaned dried shrimps.

Preparation Time: 5-10 minutes
Cooking Time: 0-5 minutes

तोंडाक ALSANDE TONDAK

Cow-peas in Brown Gravy

Tondak or tonak is the term that is usually used to describe an accompaniment but in the case of this Alsande preparation, I think it's because it makes your mouth water. Unique to the Konkan coast, Alsandes are cowpeas, which are like a cross between rajma and black-eyed peas. This vegetarian curry fills the protein requirement for the otherwise fish-eating community. If you're travelling between Konkan and Karwar, you're sure to find this lovely preparation served as a hearty breakfast dish with crusty bread like poi and pav, sometimes with the addition of shrimps.

Ingredients:

3 cups soaked cowpeas (alsande)

3 tablespoons oil

5 cloves

8 black peppercorns

1 inch cinnamon stick

1 teaspoon coriander seeds

6 dried red chillies

1 tablespoon finely chopped garlic

½ cup grated fresh coconut

2 medium onions, finely chopped

2 green chillies, slit

1 medium potato, peeled and cut into cubes

Salt to taste

2 tablespoons tamarind pulp

½ cup coconut milk

Pavs to serve

Method:

Heat one tablespoon of oil in a tempering pan, add the cloves, peppercorns, cinnamon, coriander seeds, dried red chillies, and garlic and sauté for thirty seconds.

Add the coconut and fry for a minute or till light golden. Allow it to cool slightly.

Transfer this mixture to a mixer jar, add half a cup of water and grind to a fine paste.

Heat the remaining oil in another kadai, add the onions and green chillies and sauté till the onions turn translucent.

Add the cowpeas, potato cubes, and one cup of water and mix. Cover and cook for ten minutes.

Add the salt, ground paste, tamarind pulp, and half a cup of water and cook further for ten minutes or till the cowpeas become soft.

Add the coconut milk and simmer for five minutes or till the gravy thickens.

Serve with pav.

Preparation Time: 6-7 hours
Cooking Time: 25-30 minutes
Serves: 6-8

Mushroom Stir-Fry

अळंबी

ALAMBI

SUKKE

Alambi is a type of indigenous mushroom that grows wild and free in this part of the coastal belt. If you're ever taking a road trip from Konkan to Karwar you're sure to spot tribal women selling these wonderful morels wrapped in large leaf packets or vatta. The reddish-brown mushrooms have a unique earthy flavour quite different from button mushrooms. Locals thrive on them during the monsoon months and use them in a variety of preparations spanning across courses. I'm sharing the Alambi Sukka recipe because I find it brings out the textures and rustic taste of these wild mushrooms brilliantly. They also taste splendid when masala fried, like prawns, but that's a recipe for another time...maybe another book!

Ingredients:

20 Goan mushrooms (Alambi), quartered

2 tablespoons coconut oil

4 dried red chillies

1 teaspoon coriander seeds

¼ cup grated fresh coconut

1 teaspoon tamarind pulp

1 medium onion, chopped

1 teaspoon ginger-garlic paste

½ teaspoon turmeric powder

Salt to taste

Chopped fresh coriander leaves for garnish

Method:

Heat 1 tablespoon coconut oil in a pan. Add dried red chillies and coriander seeds and sauté till fragrant. Add coconut and sauté till golden. Take the pan off the heat and allow to cool.

Grind together the spices-coconut mixture and tamarind pulp with some water to a coarse paste.

Heat remaining coconut oil in another pan. Add onion and sauté till golden. Add ginger-garlic paste, mix and sauté for 30 seconds. Add prepared paste, mix and cook for a minute.

Add mushrooms and turmeric powder and mix well. Reduce heat to low, add little water, mix and cook till mushrooms are done (about 5 minutes).

Add salt, mix and cook for a minute.

Garnish with chopped coriander and serve hot.

Preparation Time: 5-10 minutes
Cooking Time: 10-15 minutes
Serves: 4

Since Goan mushrooms are seasonal, if you are unable to find them then you can easily substitute them with 10-12 button mushrooms.

If you've been to Goa, you've been tempted to order a portion of Goan Chilli Chicken, which is literally on every shack and restaurant menu in India's favourite holiday state. This recipe marries all my favourite things about different versions I've had over the years. I promise, each bite will transport you to a beach in Goa, where you have the sea at your feet, a beer in your hand and of course some fabulous Goan Chilli Chicken by your side.

Ingredients:

750 grams boneless chicken, cut into cubes

4 green chillies, slit

½ teaspoon cumin seeds

1 teaspoon coriander seeds

1 inch cinnamon stick

4 cloves

4 green cardamoms

2 tablespoons butter

1 tablespoon ginger-garlic paste

4 tablespoons tomato puree

1 teaspoon red chilli powder

½ teaspoon sugar

1 tablespoon vinegar

Salt to taste

1 small green capsicum, diced

1 medium onion, roughly diced

1 medium tomato, diced

Chopped fresh coriander leaves

Method:

Dry roast the cumin seeds, coriander seeds, cloves, cinnamon and green cardamoms in a pan till they turn fragrant. Allow it to cool, transfer to a mixer jar and grind to a fine powder.

Melt butter in a kadai. Add the ginger-garlic paste and sauté for a minute. Add the chicken and sauté on high heat for one minute. Add very little water, mix, cover and cook for four to five minutes on medium heat.

Add the tomato puree, mix and sauté on high heat for one minute. Add the ground powder and red chilli powder and mix well. Cover and cook for two to four minutes.

Add the sugar, vinegar, and salt and sauté for a minute. Add the capsicum, onion, tomato and green chillies and sauté on high heat for three minutes or till the mixture is dry.

Garnish with chopped coriander and serve hot.

GOAN CHILLI CHICKEN

Preparation Time: 5-10 minutes
Cooking Time: 15-20 minutes
Serves: 6-8

PRAWN KALWAN

Malwani Prawns Curry

The word Kalwan is actually derived from the action of mixing - in this case rice and curry. The spice mix that goes into it is the famous Malwani masala. This is a recipe that everybody has their own versions of - something I learnt after eating at different 'khanavals' in my hometown where every Prawn Kalwan had its own imprint on the flavour. This one is mine.

Method:

To the prawns, add the turmeric powder and salt, mix and set aside to marinate for five minutes.

Heat one tablespoon of coconut oil in a pan. Add the coriander seeds and sauté till fragrant.

Add the broken dried red chillies and sauté for a minute. Add half the onion and sauté till golden.

Add the coconut, mix and roast for thirty seconds. Take the pan off the heat and add the rice and mix well. Allow the roasted mixture to cool slightly.

Grind the roasted spice-coconut mixture along with some water to a fine paste.

Heat the remaining oil in another pan. Add the remaining onion and sauté on high heat till it turns golden.

Add the garlic and sauté till golden. Add the ground paste, mix and cook for a minute.

Add the marinated prawns, mix and cook for a minute.

Reduce the heat to low, add the Malvani masala and mix well. Add some water, mix and cook on low heat for five minutes.

Add the coconut milk and mix well. Add the kokum petals, mix and cook on low heat for two to three minutes. Serve hot.

Ingredients:

1 cup medium prawns, shelled and deveined with tails intact

½ teaspoon turmeric powder

Salt to taste

2 tablespoons coconut oil

1 teaspoon coriander seeds

4 dried red chillies, broken

1 small onion, finely chopped

¼ cup grated fresh coconut

1 teaspoon Malvani Masala (pg no 152)

1 teaspoon rice

1 tablespoon chopped garlic

½ cup coconut milk

3-4 kokum petals

Preparation Time: 10-15 minutes
Cooking Time: 15-20 minutes
Serves: 4-5

Raw Jackfruit cooked with Prawns

फणस

FANAS KOLAMBI BHAAJI

Raw jackfruits have gained a worldwide reputation of being a great substitute for meat mainly because of the meaty texture it has once cooked. In this part of the world jackfruits are easily available and seen in every type of preparation from dals and curries to snacks and starters. The combination of prawns and jackfruit in this dish creates a faux 'surf & turf' vibe. Add it to a dal chawal combo and you have a sure shot hit at hand.

Ingredients:

400 grams raw jackfruit, cut into 1 inch pieces, boiled and drained

100 gm medium prawns, shelled and deveined

½ teaspoon turmeric powder

1 teaspoon red chilli powder

1 teaspoon tamarind pulp

2 tablespoons oil

1 tablespoon minced garlic

3 green chillies, finely chopped

2 medium onions, finely chopped

½ teaspoon black pepper powder

1 teaspoon cumin powder

1 teaspoon coriander powder

½ cup grated fresh coconut

2 tablespoons chopped fresh coriander leaves

Salt to taste

Method:

Take prawns in a bowl, add the salt, ¼ teaspoon turmeric powder, red chilli powder and tamarind pulp and mix well. Set aside to marinate for five minutes.

Heat oil in a non-stick pan, add the garlic and sauté till pink, add the green chillies and sauté further.

Add the onions and cook till translucent. Add the marinated prawns and mix well. Add a little water, cover and cook on simmer for two to three minutes.

Roughly mash boiled jackfruit pieces on a plate. Add the pepper powder, cumin powder, coriander powder and remaining turmeric powder, salt and mix well.

Add to the prawns and mix well.

Cover and cook on simmer for two minutes.

Add the fresh coconut and chopped coriander and mix well. Serve hot.

Preparation Time: 10-15 minutes
Cooking Time: 15-20 minutes
Serves: 4-5

KOLAMBI कोलंबी BHAAT

Prawns Pulao with Coconut Milk

For the Konkanis, Kolambi Bhaat is home. The flavours of fresh prawns and creamy coconut running through each grain of flavourful rice... In my growing up years, it used to be a treat that would bring some respite to otherwise vegetarian mid-week meals. This recipe is one that has been tried, tested and enjoyed by everyone in my circle and I promise you too will fall in love with these simple, homely yet magical flavours.

Method:

Combine the prawns, salt, turmeric powder, and red chilli powder in a bowl. Set aside to marinate for ten to fifteen minutes.

Heat the oil in a non-stick pan. Add the bay leaf, cloves, peppercorns, cinnamon and mace and mix well.

Add the ginger-garlic-green chilli paste and sauté. Add the onion and sauté till it turns translucent.

Add the tomato, mix and sauté till it turns soft. Add the rice, mix well and cook on high heat for a minute.

Add the marinated prawns and mix well. Add the coconut milk and mix again.

Add 3 cups boiling water, stir to mix and add the salt. Mix well, cover and cook till the water evaporates and the rice is cooked completely.

Garnish with chopped coriander and serve hot.

Ingredients:

1 cup medium-sized prawns (kolambi), cleaned and deveined

2 cups Basmati rice, washed

½ cup coconut milk

Salt to taste

½ teaspoon turmeric powder

1 teaspoon red chilli powder

3 tablespoons oil

1 bay leaf

3-4 cloves

8-10 black peppercorns

1-inch cinnamon stick

1 mace blade

1 tablespoon ginger-garlic-green chilli paste

1 medium onion, chopped

1 medium tomato, chopped

2 tablespoons chopped fresh coriander leaves

Preparation Time: 10-15 minutes
Cooking Time: 20-25 minutes
Serves: 6-8

BANGDA WITH तिरफळ TIRPHAL

Baked Spicy Mackerels

Every place has a few native ingredients that give a sense of pride to the people and a unique taste to their culinary preparations. In the Konkan region, it is Triphal, a spice which for lack of a better example, is quite close to Sichuan peppercorns - almost like a coastal, earthier version of them. The fresh green Triphal is dried till black and used to flavour many dishes, especially oily Omega 3 rich fish preparations like sardines and mackerel. The flavour profile of Triphal is very unique and in this recipe (, turmeric leaves add a nice aroma and flavour that complement the Tirphal rather than overpowering it.

Ingredients:

4 whole mackerels (bangda), cleaned

20 tirphal, soaked in ¼ cup water

Salt to taste

½ teaspoon turmeric powder

½ teaspoon red chilli powder

¾ cup grated fresh coconut

1 teaspoon coriander seeds

6 dried red chillies

2 fresh turmeric leaves, halved

10-12 kokum petals

2 tablespoons coconut oil

Method:

Make slits on the surface of the mackerels. Apply the salt, turmeric, and red chilli powder and keep aside.

Preheat the oven at 200°C.

Grind together coconut, coriander seeds and dried chillies along with some two tablespoons of water to a fine and thick paste.

Apply the paste to the mackerels, add the tirphals and kokum petals and wrap them individually in turmeric leaves along with the mixture. Drizzle with coconut oil and arrange them in a baking dish.

Bake the mackerels for ten to fifteen minutes.

Serve.

Preparation Time: 10-15 minutes
Cooking Time: 10-15 minutes
Serves: 4

This preparation is locally called as 'Bangda Dhodak' where this fish is roasted in the clay oven.

RAWAS AMBAT TIKHAT

Indian Salmon in sour and spicy gravy

In our language, 'ambat' means tangy and 'tikhat' means spicy - this recipe is a wonderful culmination of these flavours. Living upto the name - vinegar, kokum and tamarind add a sour, tangy taste to it whereas the spice comes from Xepda Mirsang chillies, another indigenous ingredient from the Konkan coast. Inspired from flavours of a Goan Portugese kitchen, this curry, unlike most coastal curries, doesn't use any coconut. It's easy to make yet packed with flavours.

Ingredients:

4 medium-sized darnes of rawas

Salt to taste

¼ teaspoon turmeric powder

4 dried red chillies (2 Kashmiri, 2 byadgi)

4-5 black peppercorns

½ teaspoon cumin seeds

3 cloves

1 medium onion, chopped

½ inch ginger

6 garlic cloves

1 tablespoon vinegar

4-5 kokum petals, soaked in ¼ cup water

2 tablespoons coconut oil

1 tablespoon tomato puree

1 teaspoon sugar

Method:

Marinate the fish with salt and turmeric powder for four to five minutes.

Grind together dried red chillies, black peppercorns, cumin seeds, cloves, ½ the onion, ginger, garlic, little water and vinegar into a fine paste.

Heat coconut oil in a pan. Add the remaining onion and sauté till golden.

Add the ground paste and tomato puree and mix well. Sauté for a minute.

Add half a cup of water, mix and bring the mixture to a boil.

Add the marinated fish, mix lightly and cook for two to three minutes. Add the sugar and one-fourth cup of water and stir to mix well.

Add the soaked kokum mixture, mix and simmer for 2-3 minutes. Serve hot.

Preparation Time: 10-15 minutes
Cooking Time: 10-15 minutes
Serves: 4

You can use six Xepda Mirsang chillies instead of 2 kashmiri and 2 byadgi chillies

Other than Varan and Toi, dal preparations in my kitchen usually have some veggies added to them. Everything from brinjal to turnips works, but the one I like best is with drumsticks, which is why I am sharing this recipe. Making Shengyachi Dal always takes me on a trip down memory lane right to the magnificent moringa tree in the backyard of our house in Shiroda. Even though I do feel it's hard to match the taste of fresh drumsticks and green chillies picked from your own backyard, Shengyachi Dal is still a win-win situation thanks to all the antioxidants and nutrients it is loaded with. In fact, not just the drumsticks, we even eat the leaves and flowers that have medicinal properties. Moringa is not called a 'miracle tree' for nothing!

SHEVGASHENG DAL

Dal with Drumsticks

Ingredients:

1 cup split pigeon peas (tur dal), pressure cooked

2 drumsticks (sheng), scraped and cut into 2-inch pieces

1 small onion, finely chopped

3 green chillies, chopped

½ teaspoon turmeric powder

2-3 tablespoons chopped fresh coriander leaves

Salt to taste

¼ teaspoon asafoetida (hing)

1 teaspoon tamarind pulp

2 tablespoons grated fresh coconut

Method:

Heat the cooked tur dal in a deep pan.

Add the drumsticks, onion, green chillies, turmeric powder and chopped coriander and mix well.

Add one and half cup of water, mix and bring to boil. Cover and cook on low heat for six to seven minutes.

Add the salt, asafoetida and tamarind pulp, mix and cook till the drumsticks are fully cooked.

Add the coconut and mix well. Serve hot.

Preparation Time: 10-15 minutes
Cooking Time: 8-10 minutes
Serves: 4

A welcome change from the usual vegetable biryani, this one is much easier to make but still has plenty of oomph. Mushrooms and soya add a pseudo meaty texture and protein while coconut milk adds that quintessential coastal touch. I remember hosting a Goan themed dinner party at home, where the eternal debate of 'Is veg biryani really biryani, or just pulao?' was put to rest by the flavours of this preparation.

Mushroom and Soya biryani

जुगाड

JUGAAD BIRYANI

Preparation Time: 25-30 minutes
Cooking Time: 35-40 minutes
Serves: 6-8

Method:

Bring water to a boil in a deep pan, add the bay leaf, black cardamoms and salt and bring to a boil.

Add the rice and cook till the rice it is three-fourth done. Drain and keep aside

Heat 1 tablespoon ghee in a non-stick pan, add the cinnamon, green cardamoms, cloves, mace and sauté for half a minute. Add the onion and sauté till translucent. Add the mushrooms and soya chunks and mix well.

Add the red chilli powder, turmeric powder, coriander powder, cumin powder and salt and mix well. Add the tomato puree and mix well. Add the coconut cream and mix well.

Add the yogurt and sauté for two to three minutes. Add half a cup water and cook for two minutes.

Sprinkle half of the fried onions, mint leaves, coriander leaves, green chillies, and drizzle lemon juice. Spread the rice on the top. Drizzle saffron and remaining ghee.

Cover the assembled biryani with a tight-fitting lid and seal the edges with dough. Cook for fifteen to twenty minutes.

Serve hot garnished with remaining fried onions.

Ingredients:

10-12 button mushrooms, halved

1 cup soya chunks, soaked for 25-30 minutes and drained

2 cups rice, washed

1 bay leaf

4 black cardamoms

Salt to taste

3 tablespoons ghee

1 inch cinnamon stick

3-4 green cardamoms

6-8 cloves

1 mace

1 medium onion, finely chopped

1 teaspoon red chilli powder

¼ teaspoon turmeric powder

1 teaspoon coriander powder

1 teaspoon cumin powder

½ cup tomato puree

½ cup coconut cream

½ cup yogurt

1 cup fried onions

2 tablespoons roughly chopped fresh mint leaves

2 tablespoons roughly chopped fresh coriander leaves

4 green chillies, slit

1 tablespoon lemon juice

A few strands of saffron, soaked in milk

Whole wheat dough for sealing

आंबोळी

Savoury Pancakes **AAMBOLI**

The Maharashtrian equivalent to South Indian dosa, Aamboli is a rice pancake made with fermented batter and enjoyed for meals from breakfast to dinner and everything in between. Using a cast iron pan or bidacha tawa will give you the perfect Aamboli - slightly crispy at the bottom but with a soft, almost lacy texture on top. The recipe is easy, but making it is an art. An art that my grandmother who would dish out Aambolis at lightning speed during family meals, had mastered like no one else I know!

Ingredients:

1½ cups Kolam rice, wash and soak for 5-6 hours

½ cup split skinless black gram (dhuli urad dal)

2 tablespoons split Bengal gram (chana dal)

¼ teaspoon fenugreek seeds (methi dana)

½ cup flattened rice (poha)

Salt to taste

Oil for applying and drizzling

Chutney or meat curry to serve

Method:

Wash and soak the skinless black gram, split Bengal gram and fenugreek seeds together for two to three hours.

Just before grinding, wash and soak flattened rice for half an hour.

Grind together all the above-mentioned ingredients along with soaked kolam rice and three-fourth cup of water to a smooth and thick paste. Set aside to ferment overnight or for six to eight hours.

Add the salt and mix well.

Heat a cast-iron griddle. Grease with a little oil. Pour batter and spread it to form a thick pancake. Cover and cook on low heat for three minutes. Flip it and drizzle some oil and cook on low heat for a minute.

Serve with chutney or meat curry.

Preparation Time: 12-16 hours
Cooking Time: 15-20 minutes
Serves: 6-8 ambolis

PATOLI

पातोळी

Coconut stuffed rice flour pancakes

Quite similar to ukdiche modak, Patoli has a plus side because of how easy they are to make. There is no fuss about getting the shape right and the added flavour of turmeric leaves is just brilliant. Smearing the fragrant leaves with a thick rice flour paste used to be the kids' contribution to the elaborate Gauri Ganpati festivities at home, besides of course eating them. To my pleasant surprise I recently found that patolis are made by a lot of Goan Christian communities too.

Ingredients:

4 turmeric leaves, halved to make 8 patolis (each half should be about 4 inch long)

1½ cups rice flour

1½ teaspoons ghee + to serve

1½ cups grated fresh coconut

¾ cup grated jaggery

1 tablespoon broken cashew nuts

1 teaspoon green cardamom powder

Method:

Heat 1 teaspoon ghee in a pan, add coconut and mix well. Add jaggery and mix till the jaggery melts. Add cashew nuts and mix. Add green cardamom powder mix and cook for three minutes on low flame, stirring continuously. Remove from heat and allow to cool to room temperature.

Combine rice flour and remaining ghee in a bowl. Add sufficient water and mix well to make a smooth and thick batter.

Spread some of the batter over the leaf, place a portion of coconut mixture on one side of the leaf, fold it lengthwise bringing the edges together. Similarly make rest of the patolis.

Heat sufficient water in a steamer, place the prepared leaves in the steamer basket, cover and steam for 10 minutes.

Serve the patolis immediately. Peel the leaves and add a dollop of ghee just before eating. (Discard the leaves)

Preparation Time: 10-15 minutes
Cooking Time: 15-20 minutes
Serves: 8

GRANDMOTHER AND MOTHER'S KITCHEN

I was born and brought up in a joint family of Gaud Saraswat Brahmins (GSB) in Matunga, Mumbai. My grandfather Janardan Patki, fondly known as Gharu anna (because of his light eyes) was a

renowned architect of yesteryear Mumbai. As a consequence, our house Ganesh Bhuvan, was wonderfully designed and, big enough to comfortably accommodate a family of fifteen.

My grandmother, Sushilabai or aaji, had the keys to the kitchen and everything went as she said. She governed and orchestrated Anant Mama, our cook, who followed her recipes and produced classical GSB style food daily. On Mondays and Thursdays, we ate vegetarian food, often without onion and garlic, but on other days seafood dominated the menu. My aaji loved the idea of a community kitchen. She would rope in all the women of the house and allot everyone kitchen duties, especially during poojas, Diwali and Bhaubeej! I for one absolutely loved being given any task in the kitchen. Things like peeling and mashing boiled potatoes for vadas, shelling green peas to make usal or adding finishing touches to a karanji with a cutter, were the little kitchen chores that gave me a sense of accomplishment!

I was never really expected to cook, but the time I spent observing and learning in my aaji's kitchen helped in my making! She instilled love for food and a sense of community in everyone, and that continues to date! So even when the family grew and scattered for want of space, the concept of community cooking remained an integral part of our lives.

When I was three, my brother, my little sister and my parents moved to our other home, Sita Sadan in Sion. Here we lived with my eldest uncle,

Vasant kaka and his family and my eldest aunt Vineeta Patkar or aatya and her family. Everyone had separate flats on different floors and different kitchens too, but the food was always a big party of deliciousness!

My mother or Aai, Manda Patki nee Muzumdar came from a Karwari family in North Canara district, South of Goa. She is a culinary genius in her own right. For example, she'd churn out a variety of preparations with just rice flour, a staple ingredient in her home in the Karwar belt. From comforting vegetarian breakfasts like thalipeeth and divshis to snacks like biscoot ambodes, my mom introduced me to many traditional yet unfamiliar dishes that are hidden treasures and little known even today. She loved cooking for people and her social circle reciprocated the love by licking their plates clean and showering her with praises every time we hosted them for a meal. Her kolambi pickle was so famous, Aai once made twenty-five little jars for all the guests at a dinner party to take home! The happiness on their faces was palpable because they knew with that prawn pickle jar, the party would continue back home too! My mother could make many dishes, but pickles were her forte and she learned that art from her mother, my grandmother Aauda Akka. Aauda Akka's kitchen in Hindu Colony, Matunga was a very traditional one. She used old school

utensils like a vili, which is a sharp curved steel blade with a coconut scraper at one end and a vegetable cutter at the other. She had cast iron pans to make dosas and vellafes and earthen pots for slow-cooked fish curries and stir-fries, which gave them a unique flavour. I loved how she would carefully remove the flesh or mashta from clamshells and delicately mix them with rice flour and spices before deep-frying them to make tisrya vade or clam fritters. Oh! And I also remember burning my tongue every time as I ate them right off the kadai!

Another dish that I won't forget, partly because nobody lets me, is her signature dish - a tender raw mango pickle that she made and sent to a bunch of friends and relatives for many, many summers! I have shared the recipe here *(pg no 52)* and I know all of you who try it will add to the list of people who thank her for coming up with such deliciousness.

NEELA KAKI

As kids, the real party for us would be a pooja because that's where all the best food would be. While every other festival was celebrated in our Matunga house, Rushi Panchami was always at the Sion home, at Vasant kaka and Neela kaki's house to be more precise. Neela kaki had gone to catering college which was a big thing back in the day and she could make every type of cuisine with ease, but the rushi chi bhaaji she made was just superb. She went through the meticulous task of sourcing, prepping and preparing a medley of mixed veggies with green chillies and coconut to make the rushi chi bhaaji served with hot, rice flour bhakris, homemade white butter, garlic chutney, sol kadhi and rice. The expertise and ease with which she cooked inspired me many years later when I started cooking properly. She was my 'Google' for any kitchen related query up till her demise in 2016. Now I'm sure she is serving up a storm in heaven too.

पन्हं

PANHA

Raw Mango Beverage

Panha is a must during haldi-kumkum celebrations that take place in most Maharashtrian households during the holy month of Chaitra. The festival or pooja is ideally meant for only married women in the household and neighbourhood, but the presence of Panha along with treats like Ambedal would make it quite a festival for us kids too. We were quite happy to take our share of chilled, sweet, tangy Panha to the terrace and spend hours playing and chatting there.

Ingredients:

2 medium raw mangoes, pressure cooked (2 whistles)

1 cup chopped jaggery

A pinch of salt

½ teaspoon green cardamom powder

A pinch of saffron, soaked in 2 tablespoons water

Method:

Peel the boiled raw mangoes, remove the pulp and transfer into a blender jar. Grind to a fine paste along with the jaggery, salt, and green cardamom powder. Transfer the blended paste into a large jar.

Add the soaked saffron and four cups of water and mix till well combined. Refrigerate for two to three hours or till chilled completely.

Pour into serving glasses and serve.

Preparation Time: 2-3 hours
Cooking Time: 0 minutes
Serves: 4-5

If the raw mangoes are not very sour then you may add the juice of one lemon to balance the tanginess.

RAGHAVDAS LAADOO

Semolina and Coconut Laddoos

It's hard for me to seperate Raghavdas laadoos from memories of my dearest ajji, who really had mastered the art of making them. She knew exactly how much we kids craved for these laadoos which is why she kept them carefully counted and sealed in a brass dabba in her custody. These were my childhood equivalent of chocolate truffles - with a firm rough coating outside but filled with the goodness of saffron and cardamom infused sweet coconut inside. Eating Raghavdas Laadoos used to always be a 'dil maange more' situation for us kids, and the grown ups in the family would often give us a bit of their share, but we rarely managed to get an extra helping from ajji.

Ingredients:

2 cups fine semolina (rawa)

1 tablespoon ghee + for greasing

1 cup sugar

2 cups grated fresh coconut

½ cup chopped raisins and almonds

1 teaspoon green cardamom powder

A generous pinch of saffron, soaked in 1-2 tablespoons warm water

Method:

Lightly roast the semolina in ghee for three to four minutes. Set it aside.

Cook together the sugar and coconut with one and a half cups of water in a kadai on medium heat till the mixture forms a single string consistency. This may take approximately six to eight minutes.

Add the chopped raisins and almonds along with green cardamom powder and saffron. Mix and cook further for one minute.

Reduce the heat to low and add the roasted semolina, mix for one minute. Switch off the heat and allow the mixture to cool slightly.

Grease your palms with a little ghee and take a small portion of the mixture and shape it into a ball/laddoo while the mixture is still warm.

You can store the laadoos in an air tight container. These laadoos stay well at room temperature for about 6-7 days.

Preparation Time: 10 minutes
Cooking Time: 20-30 minutes
Makes 16-20

Batata Vada is synonymous with Mumbai and anyone visiting the city cannot leave without tasting it. While locals have their favourites and I admit many are quite good, the best batata vada I've ever had is at a tiny highway joint called 'Ramakant' in Khopoli. It became customary for us to stop and eat garam garam batata vada at Ramakant's, while on the way to Lonavala. My father worked in the construction business, so we often travelled late in the night or in the wee hours of the morning, but it didn't matter what hour we reached Khopoli, we'd always receive a warm welcome with these piping hot batata vadas! My mother eventually managed to get the recipe from them and replicated it in her kitchen. Then, began making them as well. By sharing it in this book, I hope the recipe trickles down to your kitchen too! It is the best batata vada you will ever eat.

बटाटा BATATA VADA

Batter Fried, Spiced Mashed Potato Balls

Preparation Time: 20-25 minutes
Cooking Time: 10-15 minutes
Serves: 4-5

Adding rice flour and hot oil to the batter makes the covering of the vadas light and crispy.

Ingredients:

Vada

4 medium potatoes, boiled, peeled and mashed

Salt to taste

1 tablespoon ginger-garlic-green chilli paste

2 tablespoons chopped fresh coriander leaves

1 tablespoon oil + for deep frying

1 teaspoon mustard seeds

½ teaspoon asafoetida (hing)

1 green chilli, finely chopped

½ teaspoon turmeric powder

Few curry leaves

Batter

1½ cups gram flour (besan)

2 tablespoons rice flour

Salt to taste

½ teaspoon turmeric powder

½ teaspoon red chilli powder

1 teaspoon coriander-cumin (dhania-jeera) powder

½ teaspoon baking soda

To serve

Pavs to serve • Garlic chutney to serve • Fried green chillies to serve

Method:

Mash the boiled potatoes in a mixing bowl. Add the salt, ginger-garlic-green chilli paste, and coriander leaves.

Heat the oil in a tempering pan. Add the mustard seeds and let them crackle. Add the asafoetida, green chilli and turmeric powder and curry leaves. Sauté for a minute.

Pour this tempering over the potato mixture and combine well.

Divide this potato filling into eight to ten equal portions and shape each portion into a ball.

For the batter: mix together gram flour, rice flour, a little salt, turmeric powder, red chilli powder, coriander-cumin powder and baking soda. Add about half a cup of water and mix till a smooth and thick batter is formed.

Heat sufficient oil in a kadai. Add one tablespoon of the hot oil to the batter and mix well.

Dip each potato ball into the batter and coat well. Deep-fry a few at a time on medium heat for about three to four minutes or till they turn golden brown and crisp. Drain on absorbent paper.

Serve with pavs, garlic chutney and fried green chillies.

For the ginger-garlic-green-chilli paste, coarsely grind 1-inch ginger, along with 8 garlic cloves, 2 green chillies and 1-2 tablespoons water together.

My maternal grandmother is from Karwar which is blessed with an abundance of fresh seafood and clams are hot favourite. In this recipe, they are turned into 'vade' or shallow-fried fritters by mixing with some coarse rice flour and a few basic spices. It is one of those dishes that take hours to prep but gets eaten within minutes. The laborious task of deshelling and cleaning the maste or orange flesh from the clams deserves a big reward, which is exactly what Tisryache Vade are!

TISRYACHE VADE

Clam Fritters

Ingredients:

2 cups deshelled and cleaned clams flesh (tisrya)

½ cup grated fresh coconut

6-8 garlic cloves

1 teaspoon tamarind pulp

1 medium onion, finely chopped

2 green chillies, finely chopped

1 tablespoon grated ginger

Salt to taste

½ teaspoon turmeric powder

1 teaspoon sambar powder

2 tablespoons chopped fresh coriander leaves

½ cup rice rawa

¼ cup rice flour

Oil for shallow frying

Method:

Grind together the coconut, garlic and tamarind pulp into a coarse paste.

To this paste, add the chopped onions, green chillies, ginger, salt, turmeric powder, sambar powder, fresh coriander, clam flesh and rice rawa and mix well.

Heat sufficient oil in a frying pan.

To make the vade, take a small lemon sized portion of the mixture and shape it into a ball. Flatten them to shape like tikkis (vade). Spread the rice flour on a plate and coat the vade in it. Dust off the excess flour from the vade.

Gently place the vade into the hot oil and shallow-fry on medium heat for approximately two minutes on each side, till it turns golden brown. Serve hot with a dip of your choice.

Preparation Time: 15-20 minutes
Cooking Time: 5-10 minutes
Serves: 12-15 vadas

ANSA FANSA CHI BHAAJI

Fruits in Coconut Gravy

Fruits in a curry might sound odd at first, but one taste of this will change your mind. It has a wonderful flavour profile with tangy pineapples balancing the sweetness of ripe jackfruits and mangoes, all of which grow in abundance during Konkan summers. We never missed a chance to make this preparation for those few months and at my wedding in May 1985, we knew we must have it on the menu. Our apprehensions on whether my Kolhapuri in-laws, who are used to spicy food would enjoy eating this fruity dish were eventually put to rest when Ansa Fansachi Bhaaji became a common feature on the summer menu in my marital home too!

Ingredients:

1 cup diced pineapple (ananas)

1 cup ripe jackfruit (fanas), deseeded and cut into medium sized pieces

4 ripe small wild mangoes (ghota), peeled

2 tablespoons oil

½ teaspoon mustard seeds

¼ teaspoon fenugreek seeds (methi dana)

½ teaspoon asafoetida (hing)

½ teaspoon turmeric powder

Salt to taste

¾ cup grated fresh coconut

3-4 dried Bedgi red chillies

2 tablespoons grated jaggery

Method:

Heat the oil in a pan. Add the mustard seeds and let them crackle. Add the fenugreek seeds, hing and turmeric powder and mix well.

Add the pineapple, jackfruit, mangoes, and salt and mix. Add half a cup of water and cook for five minutes on medium heat.

Grind fresh coconut and dried red chillies with half a cup of water together to a fine paste.

Add the prepared paste into the fruits mixture, add the jaggery and half a cup of water to adjust the consistency and mix well. Cook for two minutes. Serve.

'Ghota' is a type of small ripe wild mango which is found in abundance in the western coastal region. In case of unavailability of Ghota mangoes, you can easily substitute them with 1 medium ripe mango, peel and cut them into dices.

Preparation Time: 5-10 minutes
Cooking Time: 10-15 minutes
Serves: 5-6

KARWARI

कारवारी

KAIRI PICKLE

Tender Raw Mango Pickle

A recipe that is my maternal grandmother's legacy, one that my mother and now I, hope to carry forward. My ajji's sweet gesture of sending this tangy, homemade kairi pickle to friends and relatives for several summers has given them fond memories to remember her by even decades after her demise. My memories of slitting and deseeding the tender mangoes, pounding the pickle masala and carefully filling the mix in the barnis are as strong as the shelf life of the pickle itself!

Ingredients:

- 1½ kilograms sea salt
- 3 kilograms small tender raw mangoes
- 3 tablespoons fenugreek seeds (methi dana)
- 25 grams Irani + Hira hing (asafoetida) (25 grams combined)
- Washed and cleaned mango leaves as required
- 3 inch dried whole turmeric
- 50 grams mustard seeds
- 150 grams split yellow mustard seeds (rai kuria)
- 250 grams red chili (bedgi chili) powder
- 4 cups sesame oil

Preparation Time: 20-25 minutes
Cooking Time: 10-15 minutes
Shelf life upto 1 year

Method:

Clean the tender mangos and wipe them dry.

Slit and de-seed each mango without cutting it through completely.

Stuff each mango with sea salt and arrange them in a big vessel, cover with washed and cleaned mango leaves. Place a heavy weight on them and set aside for two days indoors. Just mix them once so that all the mangoes receive equal pressure..

By the third day, all mangoes will be soaked in the brine. You can discard the mango leaves.

Place the tender mangoes on a clean cloth to dry, leaving the brine aside. Do not discard it.

Strain the brine in a pan and boil till it reduces to one-fourth of its original amount. Set aside to cool.

Heat one cup of sesame oil in a pan, add the mustard seeds, asafoetida, fenugreek seeds, and turmeric and sauté on low heat for five to ten minutes. Set aside to cool completely. Grind well in a mixer.Heat the remaining oil in another pan and let it smoke. Switch the heat off and allow the oil to cool.

Remove one cup of the oil and set aside. Add the red chilli powder, split yellow mustard seeds and the blended masala with one cup of the reserved brine.

Prepare a ceramic jar to store the pickle, add half a cup of brine in it.

Start stuffing each tender mango with the prepared masala and start layering them one by one in the jar. Alternately pour the brine till it is over.

Once the jar is full, pour reserved oil in it.

Keep the stuffed mangoes pressed in the jar so that they are fully immersed in oil. Cover with a lid, tie a muslin cloth around the mouth and the neck of the jar. It is ready to be consumed after a week. It can be stored for a year.

We make this pickle with very tender raw mangoes, available for only about a week during Ram Navami in the month of Chaitra. Try and get the most tender raw mangoes for this pickle.

RUSHI CHI BHAAJI

Mix Green and Root Vegetables

On the second day of Ganesh Chaturthi, people in the Konkan coast celebrate Rushi Panchami - a day devoted to the 'Saptarishi' or the 7 great sages who according to our mythology control the entire universe. Rushi chi Bhaaji is a must-have on this day and in the Patki household it was always Neela Kaki, who made it. She put in hours and love to make this dish. A mix of seasonal vegetables, tubers and gourds are layered on a bed of leafy greens and spiced with the right balance of flavours from coconut, green chilli and tamarind. Along with hot rice flour bhakris slathered in homemade white butter it makes a super gratifying meal.

Method:

Heat the oil in a big vessel. Add the green chillies and asafoetida. Add all leafy vegetables in it and sauté on high heat for two minutes. Add the 2 cups of water, mix, cover and cook for five minutes on medium heat.

Add the corn on the cobs and raw peanuts. Cover and cook for ten minutes on medium heat.

Add all the chopped vegetables and roots. Mix well, cover and cook for one minute.

Lastly, add the gourds as they tend to cook the fastest.

Add the salt and half a cup of water, mix, cover and cook for four minutes on low heat.

Grind the coconut and tamarind together with half a cup of water into a fine paste and transfer this into the vegetable mixture. Mix well, increase the heat to medium and continue to cook for two to three minutes or till all the vegetables are cooked completely.

Serve with bhakri and white butter.

Preparation Time: 1 hour
Cooking Time: 30-40 minutes
Serves: 10-12

Ingredients:

5 medium bunches colocasia leaves (alu), chopped

1 medium bunch sorrel leaves (ambat chukka), chopped

1 medium bunch amaranth leaves (lal math), chopped

2 medium bunches black-eyed peas leaves (chawli), chopped

2 corn cob, cut into 2-inch pieces

½ cup raw peanuts

1 amaranth stalk(dambe), cut into 2-inch pieces

1 medium raw banana, peeled and cut into 2-inch cubes

5 gongura fruit (ambade), peeled

1 large sweet potato (ratali), cut into 2-inch pieces

3 colocasia/taro (arbi), cut into half

100 grams yam (suran), cut into 2-inch pieces

100 grams red pumpkin (lal bhopla), cut into 2-inch pieces

1 medium ridge gourd (shirali), cut into 2-inch pieces

1 medium snake gourd (padwal), cut into 2-inch pieces

1 medium sponge gourd (ghosali), cut into pieces

4 tablespoons oil

10 green chillies

1 teaspoon asafoetida (hing)

Salt to taste

1 cup grated fresh coconut

3 tablespoons tamarind paste

To serve

Bhakri as required

White butter

Depending on the type of the chopped vegetables, the cooking time varies. Ensure that the vegetables are not over-cooked and mushy.

तोंडली TONDLI

DABDABIT

Ivy Gourd in Brown Masala

Dabdabit in Marathi means semi-thick gravy and that's how this preparation gets its name. You can make a Dabdabit with any vegetables of your choice - right from tubers like yam and potato to gourds like tondli (ivy gourd), shirali (ridge gourd), padwal (snake gourd) etc. The masala is usually bright orange in colour because of the dried red chillies and coconut. When made with ivy gourd, dried coconut and fried onions are used, which gives it a brownish tinge and that is the version I'm sharing with you. In my native village, Dabdabit is paired with Bhaatachi pej, which is rice kanji or porridge. Ah! The simple joys of life!

Ingredients:

300 grams ivy gourd (tondli), cleaned, ends trimmed and slit

2 tablespoons oil

2 medium onions, finely chopped

½ teaspoon turmeric powder

1 teaspoon red chilli powder

1 teaspoon garam masala powder

Salt to taste

2 tablespoons grated fresh coconut

1 tablespoon grated dried coconut

1 tablespoon tamarind pulp

1 tablespoon grated jaggery

Chapattis or rice kanji (pej) to serve

Method:

Heat one tablespoon of oil in a pan. Add half of the onions and sauté till translucent.

Add the ivy gourd and sauté for a minute. Add the turmeric powder, red chilli powder, garam masala powder and salt and mix well. Add half a cup of water, mix, cover and cook on low heat for eight to ten minutes.

Meanwhile, heat the remaining oil in another pan. Add the remaining onions and sauté on medium heat till dark brown.

Add the coconut and sauté for two minutes on low heat. Add the dried coconut and cook till brown. Switch off the heat and allow it to cool.

Transfer the roasted coconut mixture into a mixer jar, add half a cup of water and tamarind pulp and grind to a fine paste.

Add the ground paste into the ivy gourd mixture, add water to adjust the consistency and mix well. Add the jaggery, mix and simmer for two minutes.

Serve hot with chapattis or rice kanji (pej).

Rice Kanji Recipe - Cook ¾ cup rice in 5 cups of water on low heat till soft, for approximately 30 minutes.

Preparation Time: 10-15minutes
Cooking Time: 25-30 minutes
Serves: 4-5

काजु KAJU VATANA GOLE

Green Peas and Tender Cashew Nut Stir Fry

Green peas are not a very common sight on the west coast and Kaju Vatana Gole is one of the few recipes it is used in. Usually made during weddings and other occasions to give guests from other parts of the country something familiar to chow down on amongst all the traditional local fare. What brings this dish close to home is the addition of tender cashewnuts, which are native to the Goan belt. The cashewnut under the bright orange fruit is enclosed in a grey shell that is cracked and peeled to reach the tender cashew kernel. You can then enjoy the fruits of your labour, quite literally. Kaju Vatana Gole has a short cooking time and subtle flavour making it ideal for a quick meal.

Method:

Heat the oil in a pan and let it heat up. Add the mustard seeds and let them splutter.

Add the asafoetida, turmeric powder, curry leaves and green chillies and mix well.

Add the peas along with tender cashews and mix well

Add one-fourth cup of water, cover and cook for eight to ten minutes.

Add the salt, sugar and pepper powder, mix and cook for two minutes or till peas become soft.

Serve hot garnished with coconut and coriander leaves.

Ingredients:

1 cup peeled tender cashew nuts (kaju)

2 cups fresh shelled green peas (vatana)

2 tablespoons oil

1 teaspoon mustard seeds

½ teaspoon asafoetida (hing)

½ teaspoon turmeric powder

A few curry leaves

3 green chillies, roughly chopped

Salt to taste

1 teaspoon sugar

½ teaspoon black pepper powder

½ cup grated fresh coconut

2 tablespoons chopped fresh coriander leaves

Preparation Time: 5-10 minutes
Cooking Time: 15-20 minutes
Serves: 4-5

¼ cup tur dal, soaked for 1 hour
2 tbsp crushed garlic
¼ cup fresh grated coconut
2 tbsp black peas (kala watana)
soaked for 7 – 8 hours
1 medium sized banana flower
½ tsp turmeric powder
1 tsp chilli powder
1 tsp garam masala
¼ cup buttermilk
1 tbsp jaggery grated
3 tbsp oil

केळफुल BHAAJI

KELPHUL Banana Flower Stir Fry

Cooking with banana flowers is an art and the GSB's like the Bengalis have quite mastered it. The abundance of banana plantations along the coast make these flowers a common appearance in a Konkan kitchen. Kelphul chi bhaaji is a simple stir fry that brings out the lovely flavours and unique texture of the banana flowers perfectly. Prepping it is a labour of love, but I urge each of you to try and get your hands on some banana flowers to try this recipe, you will thank me later.

Method:

Before cleaning the kelphul or banana flower, apply oil on your palms to avoid staining your fingers.

Start peeling off the purple layers or the petals and remove the white florets.

In each floret there is a long string with a round head called 'stamen' and a translucent thin cover, which needs to be removed and discarded. Continue doing this till all the florets are removed and the central core is seen.

Finely chop the florets and the core. Soak them in buttermilk alongwith one cup of water. Set it aside for 4 -5 hours. (This is to get rid of the astringent sap.)

Drain out the buttermilk and add the chopped banana flower and core in a pan. Add tur dal, black peas, and 2 cups water. Place the pan on low heat and cook for 15 minutes or till the black peas is soft and most of the moisture is evaporated.

Heat oil in a kadai. Add garlic and sauté till it turns brown. Add the banana flower mixture, salt, red chilli powder, turmeric powder and garam masala powder. Add ½ cup water, cover and cook on medium heat for 5 minutes.

Add jaggery and mix, cook for 2 minutes. Add coconut and mix, switch off the heat.

Serve.

Preparation Time: 10-15 minutes
Cooking Time: 15-20 minutes
Serves: 4-5

TISRYA KOSHIMBIR

Clams Stir Fry

Koshimbir means salad in Maharashtrian cuisine, but this recipe is a stir-fry. I guess that it is called Koshimbir because all the ingredients, including the single shelled clams, are super fresh and quickly tossed together to create this dish. It can be eaten as a main course, but it is just as enjoyable by itself. My cousins and I would compete to see who could eat the most and declare the winner by counting leftover shells.

Ingredients:

3 cups clams (tisrya), halved

1½ tablespoons coconut oil

2 medium onions, finely chopped

Salt to taste

½ teaspoon turmeric powder

½ teaspoon red chilli powder

1 teaspoon black pepper powder

½ teaspoon garam masala powder

½ cup grated fresh coconut

2 tablespoons chopped fresh coriander leaves

2 green chillies, finely chopped

1 tablespoon finely chopped ginger

7-8 kokum petals

Method:

Heat the coconut oil in a pan. Add the onions and sauté on medium heat for two to three minutes or till they turn golden brown.

To the clams, add the salt, black pepper powder, turmeric powder, red chilli powder and garam masala powder and mix well.

Add the coconut, coriander leaves, green chillies and ginger to the clams mixture and mix well. Add this into the onion mixture along with the masala. Add two tablespoons of water and mix. Cover and cook for five minutes.

Add the kokum petals, mix and cook on medium heat till the mixture dries.

Serve hot.

Preparation Time: 10-15 minutes
Cooking Time: 10-15 minutes
Serves: 4

KONKANI CHICKEN CURRY

A Konkani-style chicken curry, is just like any other chicken curry – the epitome of comfort food. The recipe is simple and the flavours are mild, with a hint of fresh coconut milk that brings it closer to home. According to the kids in our family, who have either settled or are studying abroad, this chicken curry is what they make when they are feeling homesick. Gaurang, who has turned out to be a super-smart cook since he moved to London, makes it with canned coconut milk and it turns out just as good.

Ingredients:

750 grams chicken, curry cut

Salt to taste

2 tablespoons red chilli powder

½ teaspoon turmeric powder

1 tablespoon ginger-garlic-green chilli paste

2 tablespoons oil

1-inch cinnamon stick

4-5 cloves

1 mace blade

8-10 black peppercorns

2 bay leaves

1 star anise

2 medium onions, chopped

1 medium tomato, chopped

2 medium potatoes, peeled and cut into large cubes

1 cup coconut milk

2 tablespoons chopped fresh coriander leaves

Method:

To the chicken, add the salt, one tablespoon of red chilli powder, one-fourth teaspoon turmeric powder and half tablespoon ginger-garlic-green chilli paste and mix well. Set aside for five to ten minutes.

Heat the oil in a pan. Add the cinnamon, cloves, mace, peppercorns, bay leaves and star anise and sauté well.

Add the onions and sauté till they turn translucent.

Add the tomato, mix and cook on low heat till it turns soft.

Add the remaining ginger-garlic-green chilli paste, remaining turmeric powder and remaining red chilli powder and mix well.

Add the marinated chicken, mix well and sauté for a minute.

Add the potatoes and one cup of water, cover and cook for fifteen to twenty minutes.

Add the coconut milk and simmer for five minutes. Take off the heat.

Garnish with coriander leaves and serve hot.

Preparation Time: 15-20 minutes
Cooking Time: 30-35 minutes
Serves: 4-6

SANGAMESHWARI CHICKEN

संगमेश्वरी

Spicy Chicken Curry

Some people may enjoy scenic views on a road trip and some may enjoy the cool breeze hitting their face, but what I enjoy most about road trips is stopping at little known dhabas and roadside eateries where I have eaten some of the best meals of my life.

Sangameshwari Chicken is one such discovery we had on a road trip to Goa. In a town called Sangameshwar, near Ratnagiri where expert home chefs serve just one hero dish on makeshift cots under the shade of gigantic trees. The USP of this curry is smoky, earthy Sankeshwari chillies and a spice called nagkeshar which give this dish a unique pungent flavour. Only freshly ground whole spices are added along with a hint of Byadagi chillies for that fiery red colour. The final curry looks spicier than it tastes, so dive right in!

Ingredients:

750 grams chicken, curry cut

1½ teaspoons red Sankeshwari chilli powder

Salt to taste

1 tablespoon ginger-garlic-green chilli paste

2 tablespoons oil

1-inch cinnamon stick

4-5 black peppercorns

1 black cardamom

5 cloves

¼ teaspoon stone flower (dagad phool)

2 cobra saffron (naagkeshar)

1 tablespoon poppy seeds

½ cup grated dried coconut

2 tablespoons ghee

1 tablespoon chopped garlic

1 medium onion, chopped

½ cup coconut milk

2 tablespoons lemon juice

2 tablespoons chopped fresh coriander leaves + for garnish

Preparation Time: 10-15 minutes
Cooking Time: 20-25 minutes
Serves: 4-6

Method:

To the chicken, add the salt and ginger-garlic-green chilli paste, mix well and set aside for five to ten minutes.

Heat the oil in a pan. Add the cinnamon, peppercorns, cardamom, cloves, stone flower, nagkeshar and poppy seeds and sauté till fragrant. Add the dried coconut, mix and sauté till golden. Take the pan off the heat and allow the mixture to cool.

Transfer the roasted mixture into a mixer jar, add half a cup of water and grind to a fine paste.

Heat the ghee in another pan. Add the garlic and sauté for thirty seconds. Add the onion and sauté till golden. Add the marinated chicken and sauté on high heat for two minutes.

Add the Sankeshwari chilli powder and mix well. Add half a cup of water, mix, cover and cook on low heat for ten minutes.

Add the ground paste, mix, cover and cook for five minutes or till the chicken is almost done. Add coconut milk and cook for two minutes on low flame.

Add the lemon juice and mix well. Add the coriander leaves, mix and cook on low heat for two minutes.

KARWARI

कारवारी PRAWN CURRY

with RAW MANGO

Eating a fish curry-rice meal is the highlight of the day for most Karwari people and a Sungta (shrimps) Curry with Raw Mangoes takes things to another level. The flavours of this coconut prawn curry get an upgrade with chunks of fresh green mango. During the months when fresh mangoes are not available, dried raw mango chunks aka Ambushi is added. According to my mom, using locally produced coconuts also adds to the unique taste of the seafood curries. She says it is because the manure used to grow the trees is made mostly with fish. I doubt that this is the scientific explanation, but I certainly agree that coconuts from this area are something different!

Ingredients:

1½ cups medium prawns, peeled and deveined

1 medium raw mango, peeled and cut into 1-inch pieces

¼ cup grated fresh coconut

Salt to taste

½ teaspoon turmeric powder

4 dried red chillies

1 teaspoon coriander seeds

6 black peppercorns

2 tablespoons coconut oil

½ medium onion, finely chopped

½ cup coconut milk

Method:

To the prawns, add the salt and turmeric powder and mix well. Set aside to marinate for ten minutes.

Add the coconut to a mixer jar, add the dried red chillies, coriander seeds, black peppercorns and half a cup of water and grind to a fine paste.

Heat one tablespoon coconut oil in a shallow pot. Add one tablespoon onion and sauté till translucent.

Add the prawns and sauté for one minute. Add the ground paste, raw mango pieces and one cup of water and mix well. Simmer for five minutes.

Add the coconut milk and mix well. Continue to simmer for five minutes.

Heat the remaining coconut oil in a tempering pan. Add the remaining onion and sauté till it turns dark brown. Pour this over the prawn mixture, mix, cover and switch the heat off. Serve hot.

To make this dish in Hooman style, you can just add Cancona Mirsang dried red chillies and for the tanginess add the tamarind pulp instead of raw mango. You can also add a handful of ladies' finger or drumsticks or radish in the gravy. This will take it to the next level.

Preparation Time: 10-15 hours
Cooking Time: 15-20 minutes
Serves: 4

KALVA MASALA

Oyster in Brown Masala

The highlight of making Kalva Masala in my ancestral home would be the process of cleaning and prepping the oyster. Carving sweet flesh out of a large sackful of oysters, ensuring that the calcified chip connecting the flesh to the shell is removed is the most important part. You don't want to get that unappetizing crunch of the shell when you dig into this dish.

Ingredients:

2 cups medium-sized oysters (kalva), cleaned

3 tablespoons oil

5 black peppercorns

1-inch cinnamon stick

5 cloves

1 teaspoon coriander seeds

5 garlic cloves

5 dried red chillies

½ cup grated fresh coconut

1 medium onion, finely chopped

½ teaspoon turmeric powder

Salt to taste

1 tablespoon tamarind pulp

¼ cup coconut milk

Method:

Heat one tablespoon oil in a shallow pan, add the peppercorns, cinnamon, cloves, coriander seeds, garlic and dried red chillies till they crackle.

Add the fresh coconut and sauté for two minutes on low heat. Take the pan off the heat and allow it to cool slightly. Transfer the mixture into a mixer jar, add a little water and grind to a fine paste.

Heat the remaining oil in another pan, add the onions and sauté till translucent. Add the kalva to this and fry for a minute.

Add the turmeric powder, salt, and half a cup of water and cook on low heat for five minutes.

Add the ground paste, and tamarind pulp and mix well. Simmer for five minutes.

Add coconut milk and cook on low heat for two minutes. Switch the heat off. Serve hot.

Preparation Time: 5-10 minutes
Cooking Time: 10-15 minutes
Serves: 4

BOMBIL TIKLE

Bombay Duck (fish) in Thin Spicy Gravy

Tikle is the simplest of Konkan curries and is made in every household and demographic in the region. A poor man's curry, it is thin in consistency and made with easily available modest varieties of fish like Bombay Ducks, Silverfish, Mackerel and Sardines. The texture of bombil works brilliantly in this curry. With boiled rice, it is one of the simpler things in life which give you tons of satisfaction in each morsel.

Ingredients:

- 4 Bombay ducks (Bombil), cut into 1½ inch pieces
- 4 dried red chillies
- 1 teaspoon coriander powder
- 1 teaspoon cumin powder
- ¼ teaspoon turmeric powder
- 1 teaspoon red chilli powder
- 2 tablespoons tamarind pulp
- Salt to taste
- 3 tablespoons oil
- 2 tablespoons crushed garlic
- 2 tablespoons chopped fresh coriander leaves

Method:

Dry roast red chillies for one minute. Remove from heat and allow it to cool. Put into a mixer jar, add a little water, red chilli powder, coriander powder, cumin powder, turmeric powder, and tamarind pulp and grind to a fine paste.

Take bombil in a bowl, add the salt and mix well. Set aside for five minutes.

Heat oil in a pan. Add the garlic and sauté for two minutes.

Add the ground paste and mix well. Add one cup of water and let it come to a boil.

Gently add the marinated fish, add three-fourth cup of water and cook for five minutes or till the oil separates.

Add the chopped coriander, mix and cook for a minute. Serve hot.

Preparation Time: 10-15 hours
Cooking Time: 8-10 minutes
Serves: 4

GSB POMFRET आमटी

AMTI

Traditional Pomfret Curry

Pomfrets are easily India's favourite seafood and this GSB-style curry does complete justice to its delicate flavour. Spiced with two types of chillies—one for colour and one for spice, this four ingredient masala makes the curry simple, smooth and satisfying. It is perfect to understand all the hype about that ultimate fish curry-rice combo people keep raving about!

Method:

To the pomfret, add the salt and turmeric powder and rub well.

Put the coconut in a grinder jar, add the raw rice, one tablespoon chopped onion, peppercorns and dried red chillies with half cup water and grind to a fine paste.

Heat the coconut oil in a pan. Add the remaining onion and sauté till golden. Add the ground paste and mix well. Add one cup water, mix and cook on low heat for a minute. Add the tamarind pulp and mix.

Add the pomfret darnes, mix lightly and cook on high heat for a minute. Reduce the heat to low and cook for two to three minutes. Add the ginger and coconut milk, mix well and cook for one minute. Serve hot.

Ingredients:

1 medium pomfret, 400 gms approx. cut into 6-7 darnes

Salt to taste

¼ teaspoon turmeric powder

½ cup grated fresh coconut

1 teaspoon raw rice

2 tablespoons finely chopped onion

4 black peppercorns

3-4 dried red chillies (2 resham patti and 1-2 byadgi), broken

1 tablespoon coconut oil

1 teaspoon tamarind pulp

½ teaspoon chopped ginger

½ cup coconut milk

Preparation Time: 10-15 minutes
Cooking Time: 8-10 minutes
Serves: 3-4

Ingredients:

- 1½ cups gram flour (besan)
- 2 small onions, finely chopped
- 2 green chillies, finely chopped
- 2 tablespoons chopped fresh coriander leaves
- 1 teaspoon chopped ginger
- 1 teaspoon turmeric powder
- Salt to taste
- ¼ cup grated fresh coconut
- ½ teaspoon black pepper powder
- 1 teaspoon red chilli powder
- 1 teaspoon coriander seeds
- 1 teaspoon raw rice
- 1 tablespoon tamarind pulp
- 1 tablespoon oil
- ½ cup thick coconut milk
- Coconut oil for drizzling

गोळ्याची GOLYACHI AMTI

Gram Flour Dumpling Curry

In North India they have Kadhi-Chawal, but in the west, we have Golyachi Amti ani Bhaat. Both have essentially the same composition but are made in our own indigenous ways. For Golyachi Amti, gram flour dumplings are not precooked or fried but boiled in the curry itself. The essence of this dish is to ensure the dumplings don't disintegrate nor do they become too hard. The trick to getting it right is to drop the dumplings when the curry is on a rolling boil. I managed to nail it the very first time I tried it in my kitchen, because of years of observing my ajji making it. You might have to make a couple of attempts to make the perfect Golyachi Amti, but it will be worth it.

Method:

To the gram flour, add one onion, green chillies, one tablespoon of chopped coriander, ginger, half a teaspoon of turmeric powder and salt and mix well. Add one-fourth cup of water or as required, to make a very soft and pliable dough.

Grind together the coconut, one tablespoon of onion, pepper powder, remaining turmeric powder, red chilli powder, coriander seeds, raw rice and tamarind pulp, and half a cup of water to a fine paste.

Heat the oil in a pan. Add the remaining onion and sauté till golden. Add one and a half cups of water, stir to mix and bring it to a boil.

Drop walnut-sized dumplings/portions of the dough into the boiling mixture, cover and cook for two minutes.

Add the ground paste, stir to mix and cook on low heat for two minutes. Adjust salt and mix well.

Add the coconut milk and cook for one minute. Drizzle coconut oil on top and add the remaining chopped coriander. Serve hot.

Preparation Time: 10-15 hours
Cooking Time: 10-15 minutes
Serves: 4

KAIRI CHI UDADAMETHI

Raw Mango Curry

Just the mention of kairi or raw mango causes a tickle down your taste buds. No matter which part of India you are from, kairi always has a special place in your heart. In my kitchen, I use raw mangoes wherever possible, from adding a sprinkle in salads to throwing in chunky slices in fish curry. This recipe has really simple ingredients, but the trick lies in getting the balance of spicy, tangy and sweet just right. After several attempts (and many tangy, delicious meals) for me, this recipe hits all the right spots!

Ingredients:

1½ cups raw mangoes, peeled, deseeded and diced

1 teaspoon split skinless black gram (dhuli urad dal)

1 teaspoon fenugreek seeds (methi dana)

1 teaspoon + 1 tablespoon coconut oil

6 dried red chillies (byadgi), broken

1 teaspoon raw rice

¾ cup grated fresh coconut

1 teaspoon mustard seeds

5-6 curry leaves

1 teaspoon asafoetida (hing)

½ teaspoon turmeric powder

Salt to taste

1½ tablespoons grated jaggery

Method:

Heat one teaspoon of coconut oil in a small pan. Add the broken red chillies, half a teaspoon of fenugreek seeds, skinless black gram and rice and sauté for a minute. Grind together the sautéed mixture and coconut to a fine paste using half cup water.

Heat the remaining oil in another pan. Add the mustard seeds, remaining fenugreek seeds, curry leaves, asafoetida and turmeric powder and let the mustard seeds crackle.

Add the raw mangoes and mix well. Add one cup of water, stir to mix, cover and cook for two minutes.

Add the salt, and mix well. Add the jaggery and mix well till the jaggery melts.

Add the ground paste, half a cup of water and mix well. Cook on low heat for two minutes. Serve hot.

Preparation Time: 10-15 minutes
Cooking Time: 10-15 minutes
Serves: 4

VALACHI KHICHADI

Field Bean Rice

When you think of khichdi you usually think of a bland, mushy mix of rice and pulses cooked together, but not this one! Valachi Khichdi is more pulao and less khichdi where field beans and fluffy rice grains are cooked together in 'Sunday Masala' to create a final dish that is well spiced and super flavourful even without any accompaniments.

Preparation Time: 15-16 hours
Cooking Time: 20-25 minutes
Serves: 6-8

Ingredients:

1 cup field beans (val), soaked for 8 hours, sprouted for 8 hours and peeled

2 cups Basmati rice, washed and set aside for 10 minutes

4 tablespoons oil

4 cloves

4 black peppercorns

1-inch cinnamon stick

1 star anise

1 tablespoon ginger-garlic-green chilli paste

1 medium onion, finely chopped

1 medium tomato, finely chopped

1 teaspoon red chilli powder

½ teaspoon turmeric powder

1 teaspoon Sunday Masala *(pg no 155)*

Salt to taste

4 kokum petals

1 tablespoon chopped fresh coriander leaves

2 tablespoons grated fresh coconut

Method:

Heat the oil in a pan. Add the cloves, black peppercorns, cinnamon, star anise, ginger-garlic-green chilli paste and onion and sauté for a minute.

Add the tomato and mix well. Add the rice and sauté for two minutes.

Add the peeled field beans and mix well. Add the red chilli powder, turmeric powder, Sunday masala, and salt and mix well. Cook for a minute.

Add four cups of boiling water, cover and cook on low heat for fifteen minutes or till the water evaporates. Add the kokum petals and mix well.

Garnish with coriander and coconut and serve hot.

ALU CHE PHATPHATE

Colocasia Leaves Curry

Leaves of Colocasia, Taro, Alu - different name, same game. This plant is the true blue (or should I say true green) example of root to stem dining. Everything from the prickly leaves to the earthy roots and tubers of colocasia is edible and once you develop a taste for it you will realise they are delicious too. In our village, the large, heart-shaped leaves are used to make patra's and the more tender leaves with black stems are used to make Alu che Phatphate or bhaaji. Use of a souring agent like tamarind or kokum is essential, not just for flavour but to neutralize the itchy effect of the leaves. Once you get past the slightly slimy texture, this dish is a pure delight. We usually make it shivrak ie., without onions and garlic when serving it as Naivedyam, but this recipe has plenty of garlic and corn cobs too!

Ingredients:

- 4 – 5 medium bunches of colocasia leaves (alu)
- 2 corn on the cobs
- 3 tablespoons oil
- 1½ teaspoons red chilli powder
- ½ teaspoon turmeric powder
- 1 teaspoon garam masala powder
- Salt to taste
- 2 tablespoons grated jaggery
- 2 tablespoons tamarind pulp
- 1 tablespoon gram flour (besan)
- 2 tablespoons finely chopped garlic

Method:

Wash the colocasia leaves and stems. Peel the stems and finely chop them. Similarly, finely chop the leaves.

Chop the corn into 1-inch pieces.

Heat two tablespoons of oil in a vessel, add the alu leaves and stir on medium heat for four to five minutes or till they reduce in volume.

Add the corn and fry for a minute. Add two cups of water, cover and cook on low heat for eight to ten minutes.

Add the chilli powder, turmeric powder, garam masala powder, salt and one cup of water and mix well. Cover and cook further for ten minutes on low heat.

Add the jaggery and tamarind pulp into it.

Mix the gram flour in half a cup of water and add it to the cooking leaves. Cover and cook on low heat for five minutes.

Heat the remaining oil in a tempering pan. Add the garlic and sauté till it turns dark brown. Add to the colocasia mixture. Cover immediately and simmer for two more minutes. Serve hot.

Preparation Time: 10-15 minutes
Cooking Time: 30-35 minutes
Serves: 4-5

Buy colocasia with tender and soft leaves with dark brown stalks for this recipe. It tastes best when had with steamed rice.

KULITH PITHALE

Horse Gram Flour Curry

Kulith Pithale Bhaat is one of the most basic, staple meals made in every household with slight variations in consistency and method. My grandmother would freshly roast and grind the Kulith on a large grinding stone or 'jaata' in our ancestral home which would fill up the entire backyard with an earthy, spicy aroma. These days, you get spiced Kulith flour easily in most markets. Horse gram gets a 10/10 for being an inexpensive powerhouse of nutrition.

Method:

Combine horse gram flour, red chilli powder, garam masala powder, turmeric powder and salt in a bowl. Add two cups of water and mix till a lump-free mixture is formed.

Heat the oil in a non-stick pan. Add the garlic and sauté till light brown.

Add the green chillies and sauté for one minute. Add the onion and sauté till translucent.

Add half a cup of water and bring it to a boil.

Add the flour mixture and keep stirring to avoid lumps. Cover and cook on low heat for two to three minutes.

Adjust the consistency by adding half a cup of water and mix well. It should be of a thin slurry consistency. Cover and cook for two minutes.

Add the kokum petals and mix well. Cover and cook for two minutes. Serve hot.

Ingredients:

¾ cup horse gram (kulith) flour

1 teaspoon red chilli powder

½ teaspoon garam masala powder

½ teaspoon turmeric powder

Salt to taste

2 tablespoons oil

10-12 garlic cloves, coarsely crushed

2 green chillies, chopped

1 medium onion, finely chopped

5-6 kokum petals

Preparation Time: 10-15 minutes
Cooking Time: 20-25 minutes
Serves: 4-6

Method:

Combine the flour, semolina and ghee in a bowl. Mix well till it resembles breadcrumbs.

Add the milk gradually and knead into a stiff dough. Cover and set aside.

Heat a pan. Add the coconut and roast for five minutes or till lightly browned. Transfer to a bowl.

Dry-roast the sesame seeds till well browned in the same pan. Add to the coconut along with powdered Bengal gram and mix well. Cool the mixture to room temperature.

Add the jaggery and green cardamom powder to the above mixture and mix well.

Heat sufficient oil in a kadai.

Divide the dough into eight equal portions, shape each portion into a small ball. Dust the worktop with some flour and roll out each ball into a medium disc.

Place a spoonful of coconut mixture in the centre, apply milk on the edges of half the disc, fold over and press the edges to make a crescent. Cut the extra edges with a karanji cutter. Similarly, make the remaining karanjis.

Gently slide in the karanjis a few at a time in hot oil and deep-fry on medium heat till light golden. Drain on absorbent paper.

Serve once cooled to room temperature.

GULACHI KARANJI

Jaggery Coconut Puffs

Sweetened with jaggery and deep fried to crisp perfection, Gulachi Karanji is a hot favourite Diwali faral. Gujiya, Ghughra, Chandrkala, Karanji - this is one dish with many aliases and names. This version is made with dried coconut instead of fresh, which automatically increases its shelf life. A brilliant example of how you don't need fancy ingredients to whip up sweet treats for yourself.

Ingredients:

½ cup grated jaggery (gul)

1 cup grated dried coconut

1 cup refined flour (maida) + for dusting

1 tablespoon semolina

1½ tablespoons ghee

Milk as required + for sealing

1 tablespoon white sesame seeds

2 tablespoons Bengal gram (chana dal), roasted and ground to a powder

1 teaspoon green cardamom powder

Oil for deep-frying

Preparation Time: 25-30 minutes
Cooking Time: 15-20 minutes
Serves: 4

भरलेली

BHARLELI

KELI

Stuffed Plantains

I can proudly say that food from my hometown has so many simple 'no-frills attached' recipes that can give many gourmet dishes a run for their money - Bharleli Keli fits the bill completely. Getting your hands on Rajali Keli, which are more like plantains than bananas, might be a bit of work, but you'll know it's worth it when you dig into the sweet-sour taste and wonderful texture it gets when cooked with jaggery and coconut. I've served this with whipped cream or ice cream as a desi version of Banana split at parties and trust me it really worked!

Ingredients:

6 ripe and firm plantains (rajali keli)

½ cup ghee

3 cups grated fresh coconut

1½ cups grated jaggery

A pinch of salt

1 teaspoon green cardamom powder

1-inch cinnamon stick

4-5 cloves

500 ml milk

Method:

Peel the plantains and cut them into two-inch pieces. Make a slit on one end of each piece for the stuffing.

Heat one tablespoon ghee in a pan. Add the coconut and sauté for one minute.

Add the grated jaggery, salt and green cardamom powder and sauté on low heat for three to four minutes or till it comes together. Take the pan off the heat and keep set to cool.

Stuff each plantain piece with the prepared mixture.

Heat the remaining ghee in another pan. Add the cinnamon and cloves and arrange the stuffed plantain pieces.

Add the milk, cover and cook on medium heat, turning the plantain pieces occasionally for even cooking. Continue to cook for ten to twelve minutes or till the mixture dries out and the plantains become soft. Serve warm.

Preparation Time: 10-15 minutes
Cooking Time: 20-25 minutes
Serves: 4-6

MOTHER-IN-LAW'S KITCHEN

While I began loving food in the kitchen in my native village and the kitchen in my mother's home, it was in my mother-in-law's kitchen that I fell in love with cooking.

From the first time I stepped into her beautiful kitchen in Kolhapur, my

mother-in-law or Aai as we fondly called her took me under her wings and treated me like a daughter she never had.

I was never meant to be the shy blushing bride from the 80s and thankfully neither Sanjay and more importantly, my in-laws, Dr Shivaji, fondly called Bhaoo and Lalita Nabar never expected that from me either.

The few days I spent with her in Kolhapur was when I learned that I had an inborn talent as far as cooking was concerned and that made me enjoy it rather than treating it as a chore.

I found it fascinating how despite being born and brought up in Belgaum, she mastered the nuances of Kolhapuri cuisine like the back of her palm.

After her marriage to my father-in-law, who had been a practising family physician in Kolhapur for many years, she moved to Kolhapur and brought all those wonderful flavours from Belgaum to make this kitchen a melting pot of culture. While she was vegetarian by choice, Aai could whip up non-vegetarian Kolhapuri delicacies that would make other women from their large non-vegetarian social circle a little insecure about their own cooking!

She introduced me to many flavours, dishes, ingredients, cooking techniques and food experiences. The first time I tasted a Kolhapuri mutton thali was with her. I still remember my eyes water and mascara run as I ate the mutton sukka and tambada rassa on the thali. I couldn't decide if it was as spicy as it was good or vice versa, so I just continued eating like every other guest in the room!

She also made the best Kolhapuri misal. Thanks to her special Kolhapuri masala, the mixed sprout gravy or katt would be red-hot and spicy. Dunking a soft piece of pav into the curry topped with crunchy farsaan, onions and a dash of lime made for the perfect bite every single time.

In fact, everything she made reflected her signature trait – simplicity. Simple but useful twists elevate the flavour in everything she cooked. For example, while making bhel, she used bhadang, which is a spicy local chivda made with short-grain, thick puffed rice instead of plain old puffed rice. Just by doing that her bhel had a whole new dimension of flavour, additional texture and of course the desired level of spice!

I remember she once took me to a gurhaal or a jaggery mill to get fresh jaggery to make puran polis. It is one of the 'sweetest food days' I spent with my mom-in-law, literally and figuratively. I was amazed to see gallons of sugarcane juice poured into a giant-sized cauldron and boiled on a huge kiln. I then tasted kaakvi which is the thick, sweetish liquid just before the jaggery is formed. We then ate sugarcane sticks and carrots dipped in this golden, semi-solid jaggery. Later that day we went back home and she made the softest, most delicate puran polis I had ever eaten! Each sweet morsel of that ghee laden puran poli made me realise how the love you put into the process of sourcing ingredients and cooking reflects in the final dish.

Besides my entire repertoire of Kolhapuri fare, the aforementioned puran poli recipe and my dearest husband, my mother-in-law gave me the confidence to break barriers of cuisine and ingredients to create food that is plain and simply delicious! It has always been my mantra in the kitchen and for that, I can't thank her enough!

KOLHAPURI JEWELLRY

If I have a long standing romance with food and I have an equally passionate love affair with jewellery! I'd always seen my mother and aunties donned in fine jewels for functions and weddings and when my marriage with Sanjay was fixed - it was my turn to be the princess!

On my wedding day, my in-laws actually made sure I did. My red silk saree was beautiful, but the show stealer was all the traditional Kolhapuri jewellery I was decked in from head to toe.

The most prominent piece amongst it all is the Kolhapuri Saaj, a long gold chain with 21 pendants - each depicting an avatar of Lord Vishnu, a chaphe kali or frangipani bud in the center and good luck charms at the end of the red or green coloured silk thread.

Then comes the Thushi which is a choker, made of small grains of gold that resemble grains of jowar. It is said that when a bride enters the house wearing a Thushi, she brings prosperity and the granary always remains full.

Tanmani is a short necklace made with pearls, red and white precious or semiprecious stones. This is always worn with the Nath, the traditional Maharashtrian nose ring made with the same jewels!

Method:

Heat four cups of water in a deep pan. Add the mixed pulses and boil for ten minutes. Strain and reserve the stock.

Heat one tablespoon of oil in a non-stick pan. Add the mustard seeds and let them crackle. Add the curry leaves, half a teaspoon of turmeric powder and asafoetida, mix well.

Add half the onions and sauté till they turn translucent. Add the green chillies and mix.

Add the boiled sprouts and mix well. Add one cup of water, stir to mix, cover and cook on low heat for five minutes.

Add the salt, red chilli powder, and garam masala powder and mix well. Add half a cup of water and mix, cover and cook for two minutes.

Add the tamarind paste and jaggery, mix and cook on low heat for two minutes. Take off the heat and set aside.

Transfer the reserved stock into a deep pan and place on heat. Add the salt, remaining turmeric powder, bring to a boil and remove from heat.

Heat the remaining oil in a small tempering pan. Add the garlic and sauté till it turns brown. Add the Kolhapuri masala, mix well and pour the tempering over the boiled stock in the pan.

Place the pan back on the heat and bring to a boil. Switch off the heat.

Place the cooked pulses in a bowl. Pour tempered stock over it and place the bowl on a serving plate. Add the chopped tomato, remaining chopped onions, chopped potatoes and chopped coriander, top with farsan.

Serve immediately with lemon wedges and pav.

KOLHAPURI MISAL PAV

Spicy lentil curry served with crunchy farsan and soft pav

To make 2 cups of mixed pulses - soak ¾ cup moth beans (matki), 2 tablespoons chickpeas (Kabuli chana), 2 tablespoons red black-eyed peas (lal chowli), 2 tablespoons small brown chickpeas (kala chana) for 6 hours.

Ingredients:

2 cups sprouted mixed pulses (matki, red chowli, Kabuli chana, kala chana)

3 tablespoons oil

½ teaspoon mustard seeds

7-8 curry leaves

½ teaspoon + a pinch turmeric powder

½ teaspoon asafoetida (hing)

2 medium onions, finely chopped

1 teaspoon finely chopped green chillies

Salt to taste

1 teaspoon red chilli powder

1 teaspoon garam masala powder

1 teaspoon tamarind paste

1 tablespoon jaggery

1 tablespoon crushed garlic

1 tablespoon Kolhapuri masala *(pg no151)*

1 small tomato, chopped

1 small potato, boiled and cubed

1 tablespoon chopped fresh coriander leaves

Farsan for topping

Lemon wedges for serving

Misal is famous across Maharashtra but most will agree that Kolhapuri misal is something else! While the base is a standard mix of sprout curry topped with farsan, chopped onions and a dash of lime, what adds oomph to the Kolhapuri version is a spicy, thin curry called 'katt' or 'tarri'. Made with garlic and a fiery hot combo of Kolhapuri Lavangi and Sankeshwari chillies, the katt has a pungent aroma and smoky flavour which hits the back of your throat, almost like wasabi. My first tryst with this spice bomb was at Phadtare Misal Centre, my husband's favourite misal joint in Kolhapur. One bite into the pav dunked in the spicy katt made my eyes water—partly because of the spice levels and partly because of how good it tasted! Teekhat misal pav has since always been my go-to snack on days when it's raining cats and dogs outside.

Preparation time: 10-15 minutes
Cooking time: 30-35 minutes
Serves: 4-5

In Maharashtrian households, upma is called Tikhat Sheera or Sanja and is made with semolina. This recipe, though similar, is Uppit, a variation made with coarse rice rawa and is popular in Belgaum, where my mother-in-law is from. Kala Vatana or black peas are added for some texture to this otherwise mushy breakfast staple. Just make sure you don't confuse rice rawa with idli rawa while making this recipe.

RICE RAWA UPPIT

Thick Porridge with Coarse Rice Flour

Ingredients:

2 cups rice rawa

3 tablespoons oil

1 teaspoon mustard seeds

1 teaspoon cumin seeds

½ teaspoon fenugreek seeds (methi dana)

½ teaspoon turmeric powder

½ teaspoon asafoetida (hing)

3 green chillies, chopped

1 large onion, chopped

2 tablespoons soaked kala vatana

Salt to taste

¼ cup scraped fresh coconut for garnish

1 tablespoon chopped fresh coriander leaves for garnishing

Method:

Heat the oil in a kadai. Add the mustard seeds and let them crackle. Add the cumin seeds, fenugreek seeds, turmeric powder, asafoetida, green chillies and onion, mix well and sauté till it turns translucent.

Add the rice rawa, mix and cook on low heat for two to three minutes.

Add the kala vatana and mix well. Add the salt, mix and cook for a minute. Add five cups of boiling water, stir, cover and cook on low heat for eight to ten minutes.

Add the coconut and coriander leaves and mix well. Serve hot.

Preparation Time: 5-10 minutes
Cooking Time: 20-25 minutes
Serves: 5-6

1 tablespoon of dry kala vatana when soaked for 4-5 hours, will give 2 tablespoons.

Ingredients:

½ cup roasted chana dal (daliya/phutana dal)

½ teaspoon ghee

1 teaspoon asafoetida (hing)

6 black peppercorns

1 tablespoon white sesame seeds

2 cups grated dried coconut

1 teaspoon sugar

A small piece of tamarind

Salt to taste

½ teaspoon red chilli powder

PHUTANA DAL CHUTNEY

Roasted Gram Chutney

I was introduced to this speciality from Belgaum by my aunt at first and then my mother-in-law, who also belong to Belgaum. Phutana Dal Chutney is quite close to South Indian podi, but the ingredients are slightly different and this one is worth a try. This roasted Bengal gram chutney is best enjoyed sprinkled over crusty local bakery bread smeared with white butter. With a cup of strong, hot filter coffee, this breakfast dish can put peanut butter sandwiches to shame.

Method:

Heat the ghee in a tempering pan. Add the asafoetida, black peppercorns and sesame seeds and sauté for a few seconds. Take off the heat and set aside.

Dry-roast the coconut on low heat for two minutes. Take off the heat and allow it to cool slightly.

Grind the coconut along with the roasted mixture, sugar, tamarind, salt and red chilli powder into a fine powder. Serve.

Store this chutney in an airtight container and it can last for ten to fifteen days.

Preparation Time: 5-10 hours
Cooking Time: 5 minutes

KHATKHATE

Mixed Vegetables in Dal

You might have tried Undhiyu, Shukto, Avial and Sai Bhaaji before, but now it's time to try Khatkhate - the GSB contribution to the collection of mixed vegetable preparations made across the country. Khatkhate or Khata is made by cooking root vegetables and gourds with dal and coconut. The only spice used is tirphal, a type of Sichuan pepper typical to this region. I love the woody aroma and pungent taste which enhances the individual flavours of the vegetables instead of overpowering them.

Ingredients:

1 cup cooked split pigeon peas (tur dal)

1 corn on the cob, cut into 2-inch pieces

½ medium carrot, cut into cubes

8-10 ivy gourd (tendli), ends trimmed and slit

8-10 French beans, stringed and diagonally cut into 2-inch pieces

100 grams red pumpkin, peeled and cut into cubes

100 grams bottle gourd, peeled and cut into cubes

2-3 colocasia (arbi), peeled and cut into cubes

1 medium raw banana, peeled and cut into cubes

100 grams yam (suran), peeled and cut into cubes

1 medium sweet potato, peeled and cut into cubes

15 tirphal, seeds removed

2 teaspoons red chilli powder

½ teaspoon turmeric powder

Salt to taste

½ cup grated fresh coconut

3 tablespoons tamarind pulp

3 tablespoons grated jaggery

Coconut oil for drizzling

Method:

Heat a pan, add the cooked split pigeon peas, corn, carrot, ivy gourd, french beans and mix well. Add half a cup of water, cover and cook for five minutes on low heat.

Add the red pumpkin, bottle gourd, colocasia, raw banana, yam and sweet potato and mix well. Cover and simmer for five minutes.

Soak the tirphal in a little water for five to ten minutes.

Add the red chilli powder, turmeric powder and salt to the vegetable mixture and mix well. Cover and cook for ten minutes or till the vegetables are almost done. Do not overcook.

Grind together the coconut and tamarind pulp along with half a cup of water into a fine paste.

Add the ground paste to the vegetable mixture, mix well, cover, and cook for two minutes.

Add the jaggery and soaked tirphal and mix well. Cover and cook for two minutes.

Drizzle coconut oil on top and serve hot.

Preparation Time: 25-30 minutes
Cooking Time: 30-35 minutes
Serves: 8-10

AMBADI CHI BHAAJI

Tempered Gongura Leaves

I'm not sure how many of you have tried Sorrel or Gongura leaves before, but for those from the Konkan coast Ambadi is a familiar name. These green leafy vegetables have a slightly tangy taste which is wonderfully balanced when cooked with coarse rice grains or kani. A fried garlic tempering or 'charcharit lasnichi fodni', as we call it in Marathi, completes the flavour profile of Ambadyachi bhaaji. Loaded with iron, zinc, folic acid and antioxidants, this recipe's roots can be traced back to my mother-in-law's maternal home in Belgaum, way before sorrel leaves were recognised as a global superfood!

Ingredients:

1 medium bunch sorrel leaves (ambadi/gongura), chopped

¼ cup soaked kala vatana

Salt to taste

½ teaspoon cumin seeds

½ teaspoon turmeric powder

¼ teaspoon fenugreek seeds (methi dana)

½ cup rice rawa

3 tablespoons oil

2 tablespoons finely chopped garlic

5 green chillies, roughly chopped

1 medium onion, finely chopped

1 tablespoon grated jaggery

Bhakri to serve

Method:

Boil the sorrel leaves in plenty of water in a pan till the leaves turn pink. Drain the water and place the leaves in another deep pan. Add the soaked black peas, three cups of water, salt, cumin seeds, turmeric powder, and fenugreek seeds and mix well. Cook on medium heat for ten minutes or till the black peas are cooked.

Add the rice rawa and mix well. Cover and cook on low heat for five minutes And take off the heat.

Heat two tablespoons of oil in a shallow pan. Add one tablespoon of garlic, green chillies, and onion and sauté on high heat for one minute. Add the sorrel-rice rawa mixture and mix well. Add half a cup of water, mix, cover and cook for two minutes. Adjust the salt, add the jaggery, mix well and cook for a minute till the jaggery melts.

Heat the remaining oil in a tempering pan, add the remaining garlic and sauté till it turns brown. Pour this immediately into the cooked vegetable. Cover and turn off the heat. Serve hot with bhakri.

3 tablespoon of dry kala vatana when soaked for 4-5 hours, will give ¼ cup.

Preparation Time: 20 minutes
Cooking Time: 25-30 minutes
Serves: 4-5

KOLHAPURI MUTTON THALI

In spite of originally being from the coastal region, Sanjay's side of the family has lived in Kolhapur long enough to call it home. After staying there for years, the customs and traditions of Kolhapur were part of the family. This included traditional Kolhapuri cuisine and for me, that was the absolute best part! Spicy, bold and vibrant - I think with the similarity of the cuisine and my personality *winks* I took to it quite immediately!

If you know anything about Kolhapuri cuisine, it won't come as a surprise that my favourite dish is Kolhapuri Thali. My suggestion for any of you who want to experience what a meat lover's Mecca is like, dive head first into a full blown Kolhapuri Mutton Thali - the synchronization of flavours and the simplicity of the preparations in it guarantee a memorable meal every single time!

The mere arrival of one at your table gives you an idea of the 'Pahunchaar' or famous hospitality of Kolhapur. A meticulously made meaty delight, all the dishes in this meal are meant to be made and eaten in tandem with each other. Whilst cooking it, you will see that all the elements align with each other and everything falls in place, almost like an A.R. Rahman song. The symphony of the cooking experience too, lingers long after you're done with it, much like the maestros' music.

The essence of this multi-course mutton thali lies in the Kolhapuri masala or chutney - a deep, red coloured masala powder that can always be kept handy in the fridge. The most basic version of a Kolhapuri Mutton Thali comprises of Sukka Mutton, Pandhra (white) and Tambda (red/spicy) Rassa served with chapatis, onions, lemon wedges and Goli Bhaat.

Now, I know the name Goli bhaat sounds rather explosive, but that's okay because the flavours really are, but the recipe, on the other hand, is quite easy. Here the 'goli' are roughly shaped mutton mince balls which are just dropped (quickly and like clock-work) into a cradle of caramelizing onions and left undisturbed till they cook and become firm. Topped with flavoured rice and served as the rice element of the meal.

All this in a basic thali and since 'basic' is not really my middle name, I am going to give you all the gorgeousness of the 'Spl. Kolhapuri Thali' which is a necessary extension on the menu of every Kolhapuri food joint - priced slightly higher and with extra perks!

This upgraded version of the regular thali has inclusions like anda sukka and a portion of spicy, tangy mutton loncha (pickle). In this book and my life, the mutton loncha recipe is inspired from the famous 'Padma Guest House' in Kolhapur. Thanks to the kind owner who years ago, graciously shared the handwritten recipe with me, which I have slightly improvised - mostly in terms of spice levels. It's a recipe that refrigerates well for a few days and can help you slowly phase out of the hangover of a meat overload mutton thali, with a simpler menu of mutton loncha and varan-bhaat the next day.

KOLHAPURI ANDA सुक्कं

Spicy Egg Masala

SUKKA

Ingredients:

4 eggs (anda), hard-boiled and peeled

1 tablespoon Kolhapuri Kanda Lasoon masala *(pg no 151)*

3 tablespoons oil

2-3 black peppercorns

2-3 cloves

½ teaspoon fennel seeds (saunf)

½ teaspoon poppy seeds (khas khas)

2 dried red chillies

½ cup + 2 tablespoons grated fresh coconut

1 teaspoon chopped ginger

1 teaspoon chopped garlic

1 large onion, finely chopped

¼ teaspoon turmeric powder

1 medium tomato, finely chopped

Salt to taste

2 tablespoons chopped fresh coriander leaves

Method:

Heat one tablespoon of oil in a pan. Add the cloves, peppercorns, fennel seeds, poppy seeds, and dried red chillies and roast for a minute. Add half a cup of coconut and roast till coconut turns light brown. Switch off the heat and set aside to cool slightly.

Grind the roasted spices-coconut mixture with some water to a coarse paste.

Heat the remaining oil in a kadai. Add the ginger and garlic and sauté till it turns light golden. Add the onion, mix and sauté on high heat till golden brown.

Add the turmeric powder, mix and sauté for a minute. Add the tomato, sauté and cook on low heat till it turns soft.

Add the ground paste, mix well and cook for a minute.

Add the salt and mix well. Add the Kolhapuri Kanda Lasoon masala, mix and cook on low heat for a minute.

Halve the eggs, add them to the pan and stir gently. Cook for one to two minutes.

Add the remaining coconut and coriander leaves and mix lightly. Serve hot.

You can make your own Kolhapuri Kanda Lasoon Masala. It is easily available in the market as well.

Preparation Time: 15-20 minutes
Cooking Time: 15-20 minutes
Serves: 4

KOLHAPURI SUKKA

मटण

MUTTON

Spicy dry Mutton

Ingredients:

1 kg mutton on bone, cut into 1-inch pieces

2 tablespoons Kolhapuri Kanda Lasoon Masala (*pg no 151*)

2 tablespoons chopped fresh coriander leaves

2 green chillies, slit

10-12 garlic cloves

1-inch ginger, chopped

4-6 black peppercorns

6 cloves

1 inch cinnamon stick

Salt to taste

½ teaspoon turmeric powder

4 tablespoons oil

3 medium onions, chopped

1 star anise

1 teaspoon coriander seeds

½ mace blade

1 teaspoon white sesame seeds

1 teaspoon poppy seeds

1 teaspoon fennel seeds

½ cup grated fresh coconut

1 bay leaf

½ cup grated dried coconut

1 teaspoon garam masala powder

Chapattis to serve

Preparation Time: 25-30 minutes
Cooking Time: 55-60 minutes
Serves: 4-6

Method:

Grind the coriander leaves, green chillies, five to six garlic cloves, ginger, two cloves, two to three black peppercorns, half of the cinnamon to a fine paste using a little water.

To the mutton pieces, add the ground paste, salt, one-fourth teaspoon turmeric powder and mix well. Set aside to marinate for ten minutes.

Heat one tablespoon oil in a deep pan. Add one chopped onion and sauté till it turns translucent.

Add the marinated mutton pieces and sauté on high heat for two to three minutes. Add two cups of water, stir, cover and cook on low heat. Intermittently add around one cup of water in total to adjust the consistency. Cook for forty-five minutes or till the mutton is three-fourth done. Strain the mutton pieces and reserve the stock.

Heat one tablespoon of oil in another pan. Add the remaining cinnamon, remaining black peppercorns, star anise, coriander seeds, cloves, mace, sesame seeds, poppy seeds and fennel seeds. Mix well and add one chopped onion. Mix and sauté till the onion turns translucent.

Add the fresh coconut, mix and sauté on low heat till it turns light brown.

Add the bay leaf and mix. Add the dried coconut, mix and sauté for two to three minutes till it turns brown.

Remove from heat and cool the mixture to room temperature.

Blend the roasted mixture into a mixer jar, add one-fourth cup of water and grind to a dry, thick and smooth paste.

Heat the remaining oil in another pan. Add the remaining garlic cloves and sauté well. Add the remaining onion and sauté till it turns light brown.

Add the ground coconut paste, mix and sauté for one to two minutes.

Add the remaining turmeric powder, garam masala powder, Kolhapuri Kanda Lasoon Masala, and salt and mix till well combined.

Add the cooked mutton pieces and mix well.

Add one-fourth cup of water and mix. Cover and cook on low heat for ten minutes or till the mutton pieces are soft. Serve hot with chapattis.

The reserved mutton stock is used for making Pandhara and Tambada Rassa (pg no. 98).

If you are not planning to make Pandhara and Tambada Rassa then you can just cook the mutton with minimum water about one and half cup, for forty five minutes on low flame.

PANDHARA KOLHAPURI पांढरा RASSA

Preparation Time: 10-15 minutes
Cooking Time: 5-10 minutes
Serves: 4-6

Lightly spiced Mutton gravy

Put the *2 cups grated fresh coconut* in a mixer jar. Add *10 black peppercorns, 1 tablespoon poppy seeds* and 1 cup water and grind to a smooth paste. ● Pour *2 cups mutton stock* (refer recipe Kolhapuri Sukha Mutton) in a deep pan. ● Strain the coconut mixture in a bowl and discard the residue. Add *1 teaspoon rice flour* and a little water and mix till well combined Add this into the mutton stock. ● Place the pan on heat and simmer for 5 minutes. Keep on stirring to avoid curdling of coconut milk. ● Add salt and mix well. Serve hot.

Heat *1 tablespoon oil* in a pan. Add *½ inch cinnamon stick, 4-5 black peppercorns, 5 cloves, 1 teaspoon white sesame seeds and 1 teaspoon poppy seeds* and sauté well. ● Add half of the *1 medium onion, finely chopped* and sauté till it turns translucent. ● Add *½ cup grated dried coconut* and sauté for 3-4 minutes. Take the pan off the heat and allow the mixture to cool to room temperature. ● Transfer the cooled mixture into a mixer jar, add 1½ cups water and grind to a fine paste. Strain the mixture into a bowl and discard the leftover residue. ● Heat the *2 cups mutton stock* (refer Kolhapuri Sukha Mutton) in a deep pan. Add the strained mixture and mix well. ● Add *1 teaspoon red chilli powder* and mix. ● Adjust the salt and mix well. Bring the mixture to a boil. This is rassa. ● To make the tempering, heat *remaining oil* in a shallow pan. ● Add *remaining onion* and sauté till it turns golden brown. Add *1 tablespoon Kolhapuri Kanda Lasoon Masala* and mix well. Put this mixture into the rassa, mix and switch the heat off. ● Serve hot.

KOLHAPURI तांबडा TAMBADA RASSA

Preparation Time: 5-10 minutes
Cooking Time: 10-15 minutes
Serves: 4-6

Fiery red Mutton gravy

Ingredients:

500 grams boneless mutton, cut into 1-inch pieces

Salt to taste

1 teaspoon ginger-garlic paste

1 teaspoon + 3-4 tablespoons oil

1 tablespoon white sesame seeds

¼ cup grated dried coconut

¼ teaspoon turmeric powder

1 teaspoon red chilli powder

1 tablespoon vinegar

2 tablespoon dried coconut slices

2 tablespoons Kolhapuri Kanda Lasoon Masala (*pg no 151*)

MUTTON लोणचे LONCHE

Mutton Pickle

Method:

To the mutton, add salt, turmeric powder and ginger-garlic paste and mix well. Set aside to marinate for ten minutes.

Heat a pan, add the marinated mutton pieces and some water and mix well. Cover with a lid and cook the mutton on low heat for thirty minutes or till the mutton is almost cooked and the moisture dries out.

Heat one teaspoon of oil in another pan, add the sesame seeds and dried coconut and sauté for a minute. Take the pan off the heat and allow it to cool. Grind this into a coarse powder.

Heat the remaining oil in a kadai, add the ground powder and sauté for twenty seconds.

Add the red chilli powder and Kolhapuri Kanda Lasoon Masala and mix well.

Add the cooked mutton pieces and mix till well combined. Cook on low heat for ten minutes or till mutton is well cooked.

Add the vinegar, dried coconut slices, and sprinkle some water to avoid burning. Mix, cover and cook for five minutes or till the mixture dries out completely. Take the pan off the heat and allow the mixture to cool completely.

Transfer the mutton lonche into an airtight container. Serve as required.

This mutton lonche can stay for two days at cool temperature or can be stored in the refrigerator for six to eight days. Warm the lonche before serving.

Preparation Time: 10-15 minutes
Cooking Time: 45-50 minutes
Serves: 4-6

KHEEMA गोळी GOLI BHAAT

Meat Ball Pulao

Ingredients:

1 cup mutton mince (kheema)

1½ cups Basmati rice, soaked for 20 minutes

Salt to taste

1 teaspoon Kolhapuri Kanda Lasoon Masala (*pg no 151*)

2 tablespoons chopped fresh coriander leaves

1 teaspoon crushed garlic

1 teaspoon finely chopped ginger

2 green chillies, finely chopped

½ teaspoon turmeric powder

½ teaspoon red chilli powder

4-5 black peppercorns

1-inch cinnamon stick

4-5 cloves

3 tablespoons oil

1 large onion, sliced

1 teaspoon ginger-garlic-green chilli paste

Pinch of garam masala powder

Method:

Mix together the mutton mince, salt, Kolhapuri masala, one tablespoon chopped coriander, garlic, ginger, green chillies, turmeric powder, red chilli powder, two to three black peppercorns, half of the cinnamon and two to three cloves in a food processor. Grind till it resembles a dough.

Heat one tablespoon oil in a non-stick pan. Add the onion and sauté till well browned.

Divide the minced mixture into 10-12 equal portions and shape each portion into a small ball. Add the mince balls into the hot oil, cover and cook for eight minutes or till cooked.

Stir lightly. Cover and cook on low heat for two to three minutes. Take off the heat and set aside.

Heat remaining oil in another non-stick pan. Add the remaining black peppercorns, cinnamon, cloves and ginger-garlic-green chilli paste and mix well. Add the rice, mix well for a minute.

Add the salt and garam masala powder and mix well. Add three cups of boiled water, stir to mix, cover and cook for two to three minutes or till the rice is half done.

Add the cooked balls with the onions and gently mix. Cover and cook on low heat for two to three minutes or till the rice is completely cooked.

Garnish with remaining chopped coriander and serve hot.

Preparation Time: 20-25 minutes
Cooking Time: 20-25 minutes
Serves: 5-6

Ingredients:

8 hard-boiled eggs

3 cups rice, soaked for 15 minutes

Salt to taste

5 green cardamoms

1 teaspoon caraway seeds (shahi jeera)

3 tablespoons oil

4 peppercorns

4 cloves

1 black cardamom

2-inch cinnamon stick

1 bay leaf

1 tablespoon ginger-garlic-green chilli paste

1 teaspoon red chilli powder

½ teaspoon turmeric powder

1 tablespoon Kolhapuri Kanda Lasoon Masala (*pg no 151*)

1 cup yogurt

A few fresh mint leaves + for garnish

1½ cups browned onions

½ teaspoon saffron, soaked in 1-2 tablespoons warm milk

Over the years of being surrounded by foodies I've found that some people are hardcore non-vegetarians and some others are reluctant and selective. It is for these hesitant meat-eaters, who probably won't enjoy Kolhapuri meaty treats as much, that the egg biryani comes to rescue. A much lighter option for a fuss-free, one-pot Sunday lunch, there isn't much more to be said about an egg biryani, the flavours speak for themselves.

KOLHAPURI EGG BIRYANI

Method:

Boil sufficient water in a deep pan. Add the salt, green cardamoms, and half a teaspoon of caraway seeds and rice. Cook till the rice is almost done. Drain and set aside.

Heat the oil in a pan, add the remaining caraway seeds, cloves, peppercorns, black cardamom, cinnamon stick, and bay leaf and sauté for a minute.

Add the ginger-garlic-green chilli paste and sauté for a minute. Add the red chilli powder, turmeric powder and Kolhapuri Kanda Lasoon Masala and mix well.

Add the yogurt, salt and mint leaves, mix and cook for two minutes.

Add six boiled eggs and half of the browned onion and mix well. Cook for a minute.

In a deep pan, alternately layer the egg mixture and boiled rice. Garnish with remaining browned onion and mint leaves. Halve the remaining boiled eggs lengthwise and place them on top of the rice mixture.

Drizzle soaked saffron on top. Cover the pan with aluminium foil and place a tawa (griddle) under the pan. Cook on low heat for ten minutes. Serve hot.

Preparation Time: 10-15 minutes
Cooking Time: 25-30 minutes
Serves: 6-8

Ingredients:

1 medium bunch
Malabar spinach (mayaloo)

¼ cup split skinless
pigeon peas (tur dal)

1 medium onion,
finely chopped

½ teaspoon
turmeric powder

1 teaspoon
sambar powder *(pg no. 153)*

Salt to taste

2 tablespoons coconut oil

4 dried Bedgi red chillies

5 black peppercorns

1 teaspoon coriander seeds

½ teaspoon raw rice

½ cup grated fresh coconut

1 tablespoon tamarind pulp

2 tablespoons minced garlic

मायाळू CHI AMTI

MAYALOO

Malabar Spinach Curry

For the longest time, I used to think Mayaloo was only available in our little coastal village and is unique to our home. Many years later I found out that Bengalis, Mangaloreans and several other communities in India are privy to this delicious leafy vegetable and they all enjoy it with equal gusto! The velvety thick leaves and the juicy fibrous stems of Malabar Spinach create a wonderful textural contrast and absorb the flavours of this curry in the best way possible. Things go a notch higher when you add clams or tiny shrimp to it. A cold rainy day, some hot boiled rice and Mayaloo Curry to go with it–this is what living the good life looks like!

Method:

Clean the Malabar spinach leaves and stems. Finely chop the leaves. Scrape the stems and cut them into 2-inch pieces.

Wash the split skinless pigeon peas thoroughly and add them to a pressure cooker. Add the chopped leaves and stems, half of the onion and two cups of water and mix well. Cook under pressure for five to six minutes. Switch the heat off and allow the pressure to settle completely.

Transfer the cooked pigeon peas and Mayaloo mixture to a deep pan, add the turmeric powder, sambar powder, and salt and mix well. Place the pan on heat and let it simmer.

Meanwhile, take one tablespoon of coconut oil in a tempering pan. Add the dried red chillies, black peppercorns, coriander seeds and raw rice and sauté for a minute. Take the pan off the heat and allow it to cool slightly.

Transfer the roasted mixture into a blender jar, add the fresh coconut and half a cup of water and blend to a fine paste.

Add the blended paste into the dal-mayaloo mixture and mix well. Cook on low heat for two to three minutes.

Add the tamarind pulp and half a cup of water and mix well. Let the mixture come to a boil.

Heat remaining coconut oil in another pan, add the garlic and sauté till it turns dark brown.

Add to the dal-spinach mixture and mix well and take off the heat. Serve hot.

Preparation Time: 10-15 minutes
Cooking Time: 15-20 minutes
Serves: 4

SANDGYACHI AAMTI

Dried Dumpling Curry

Sanjay and I got married in May 1985 and it was in the same summer that I was introduced to the almost sacred ritual of making Sandge and consequently Sandgyachi Aamti. Making Sandge, which are nothing but sun dried dumplings of ash gourd, urad dal and select spices, used to be a community activity. I remember my mother-in-law and her neighbours would spend hours making and drying these dumplings on the terrace in the summer sun. I must confess, I would often try to skip these 'Sandge sessions' for the fear of getting tanned, but I must also confess that a Sandgyachi Aamti is so good, the tan is worth it. It can give a lot of fish curries a run for their money and has definitely been a saviour during the few days of the week when we consume a vegetarian meal at home.

Ingredients:

1 cup sandge
(dried lentil and ash gourd dumpling)

½ cup grated fresh coconut

1 medium onion, finely chopped

3-4 dried red chillies

1 teaspoon coriander seeds

5-6 black peppercorns

¼ teaspoon turmeric powder

1 teaspoon tamarind pulp

2 tablespoons oil

Salt to taste

1 tablespoon grated jaggery

Method:

Grind together the coconut, one tablespoon of onion, dried red chillies, coriander seeds, black peppercorns, turmeric powder, tamarind pulp and a little water to a fine paste.

Heat the oil in a pan. Add the sandge and sauté till brown and crisp. Transfer on a plate and set aside. Add one teaspoon of onion and sauté for two minutes or till dark brown. Add the ground paste, and half a cup of water and mix well. Stirring continuously on low heat to avoid curdling.

Add the salt and mix well. Cook for a minute.

Add the fried sandge and the remaining onion and mix well. Add one-fourth cup of water and cook on low heat for two to three minutes.

Add the jaggery and mix well. Cook further for a minute. Serve hot.

Preparation Time: 10-15 minutes
Cooking Time: 8-10 minutes
Serves: 4

This recipe is just another one of my mother-in-laws' brilliant kitchen experiments and a delicious way to use up tons of sugarcane juice that would be sent to our house after the seasonal harvest. It won't be wrong to compare the flavours of these poleys with a classic pancake and maple syrup combo. Eating it always amazes me at how three simple ingredients and a hint of thinking outside the box can create something so rewarding for your taste buds. If you enjoy sweet breakfasts, it's worth going out and getting some sugarcane juice to try this recipe.

Ingredients:

3 cups sugarcane juice (usaacha ras)

2 cups kolam rice

½ cup grated jaggery

1 cup grated fresh coconut

Ghee for greasing + for drizzling + to serve

A pinch of salt

Method:

Wash the rice thoroughly and soak it in sugarcane juice for two hours.

Add the rice along with some of the sugar cane juice into a mixer jar. Add the fresh coconut and grind till it forms a fine paste. Transfer this into a bowl, add the jaggery, salt and add the remaining sugarcane juice and mix till it forms a dosa batter-like consistency. Cover and let it ferment for eight hours.

Heat a griddle. Grease it with ghee and pour a ladleful of the batter on it and spread it evenly like a pancake. Cook on low heat for two minutes, flip it, drizzle one teaspoon of ghee and continue to cook further till it becomes golden brown. Serve with ghee.

USACHYA RASACHE POLEY

Sugarcane pancakes

Preparation Time: 10 minutes
Cooking Time: 10-15 minutes
Serves: 12-15

KAKDICHA

काकडीचा

Cucumber Cake

DHONDAS

If you want to have your cake and eat it too, Dhondas is what you should make because it's delicious and free of any refined flour and artificial sugar. Made with large, wild cucumber called tausal this cake is often referred to as 'Tausali', along the coast. Traditionally it would be baked in a chulah, which adds to the wonderful flavour of the turmeric leaf parcel that enclosed it. It was my Neela kaki who mastered this Dhondas recipe in a regular oven. It's safe to say now I have too!

Ingredients:

2 cups peeled and grated large wild cucumbers (tausali)

1 cup rice rawa

¼ cup ghee + to serve

1 cup finely chopped jaggery

½ cup grated fresh coconut

10 cashew nuts, soaked

1 teaspoon green cardamom powder

¼ teaspoon baking soda

A pinch of salt

2 turmeric leaves, quartered

Method:

Preheat the oven at 180°C.

Heat two tablespoons of ghee in a pan. Add the rice rawa and sauté for two minutes. Add the grated cucumber along with its juice, add the coconut and mix well. Cook for two minutes. Take the pan off the heat and allow it to cool.

Add the jaggery, cashews, green cardamom powder, baking soda, and salt and mix well.

Grease a 10-inch baking tray with remaining ghee. Place two pieces of turmeric leaves at the bottom and pour the prepared mixture in it and spread it evenly.

Place the remaining turmeric leaves on the top and bake the mixture for thirty minutes or till golden brown.

Remove the baking tray from the oven and allow it to cool slightly. Cut into pieces and serve with ghee.

Preparation Time: 10-15 minutes
Cooking Time: 35-40 minutes
Pieces: 10-15

You might wonder why know-how of GSB history is included in this recipe memoir, but this little lesson in history will help you understand the culinary diversity in this book through a geographic lens and be a part of my food journey with ease. So here goes!

The history of GSB or Gaud Saraswat Brahmins is a record of their struggle for existence over many many centuries. A struggle that dates back to when the Aryans from Central Asia migrated to the Indian subcontinent and settled along the banks of the mystical Saraswati river in what is now Punjab and Rajasthan. this community derived their name from the great sage and their spiritual leader, Saraswat Muni who also resided on the banks of the Saraswati river. Along the fruitful banks of the river, this community thrived. They took to farming and cattle grazing and gave education a lot of importance.

By 1000 BC, as the glaciers which were the source of the River Saraswati depleted, the river began to dry out and ultimately became non-existent or hidden, like it continues to remain to date. The area around became arid and life for the Saraswats became difficult.. With the land unsuitable for agriculture and no river to fish out, the story of the migration of Gaud Saraswat Brahmins began. This migration happened over centuries across three directions along the existing river routes – in the south-west towards Sind, in the north towards Kashmir and in the east towards Bihar. In the south-west, they followed the course of river Saraswati and went up to Dwaraka and then by ship to Goa. The Saraswats who moved south-east mainly followed the Ganges.

A few years later, political upheaval made Gaud Saraswats move further eastwards to Bengal and along the river Godavari to Nashik and Goa. Even later, in the 11th and 12th century AD, the community continued to migrate - in search of better opportunities and for trade.

They spread from Goa to many parts of Maharashtra like Mumbai, Kalyan, Kolhapur, Thane and to Mangalore, Bhatkal, Dharwar, Belgaum and Honavar in Karnataka. Infact GSB's even have a strong presence as far south as Kerala and Calicut.

Multiple migrations of the GSBs from one region to another had a tremendous effect on their culinary habits. Their food spectrum evolved into a huge variety of culinary creations using indigenous ingredients from the different areas they settled in. What remains common in most parts is the predominance of seafood in their diet. Legend has it that the Saraswat Brahmins were awarded a boon of eating fish in order to avoid starvation. Which is why we still refer to fish as samudra fal or gift from the sea. It won't be wrong to call us pesco vegetarian because for us seafood is always the crux of the meal. So much so that in my home in particular, on days when we don't eat fish, we make vegetarian food to replicate the flavours!

The Gaud Saraswat community also relies heavily on coastal ingredients like coconuts, tropical fruits like pineapples and mangoes and some unique ingredients like Triphal and Kokum to flavour our food. No matter which part of the country we move to, these small, delicious things keep us rooted to our culture and rich culinary heritage. Our food is so varied and diverse, yet it has a common thread running through the flavours of every morsel. Through this book, I hope I do justice to this Big Bang of ever-evolving flavours and the glory of its roots!

MY KITCHEN

The kitchen in my current home in Vile Parle Mumbai, where I have spent more than 35 years is rightfully what I can call 'My Kitchen' This is where for the first time I had full control and was the sole person responsible for feeding the family of 3 which included my then infant son. The first time I cooked in this

kitchen, which eventually became my sacred space, was for a pooja during my post wedding functions. There is an Indian custom that when a new bride enters her marital home for the first time, she knocks over a pot of uncooked rice with her right foot. As the grains of rice scatter, they symbolize the abundance and prosperity the bride brings with her to her new home. I was an enthusiastic bride and I knocked over the pot with great gusto, scattering the rice far and wide. However, my gusto whimpered and disappeared into a corner when it was time to cook some rice!

My mother-in-law, who was busy preparing for one of the rituals, casually asked me to cook some rice and dal in the cooker. I walked into the kitchen, held the cooker in my hand and stared at the jars of dal and rice in confusion. That's when it struck me that while I had spent a large part of my life in the kitchen - watching and observing, I'd never really cooked. Sensing my confusion and reading my expression, the maid who was washing vessels by the sink came to my aid and showed me how to set the pressure cooker to make the most basic dish of Varan Bhaat. She told me the correct amount of water, the right number of whistles and the perfect heat to ensure your dal chawal turns out perfect every time. Making this Varan Bhaat was actually the beginning of my cooking chronicles. My husband, who is a man of simple tastes, always says that while masale bhaat, fish curries and biryani can satisfy your tastebuds, a good varan bhaat can satisfy your soul. The day I think I finally mastered the art of making Varan Bhaat was for my son's 'Ushtavan' ceremony. On this day I just had to ensure that the first meal Gaurang ate had the perfect balance of nutrition and flavour profiles as expected. Considering the foodie Gaurang has grown to become, I think I did quite well with that first Varan Bhaat meal.

This was just the beginning of my cooking journey, my professional food journey began in 2010 when I got a freak chance to showcase 2 of my recipes in a Marathi Food Show 'Aamhi Saare Khavayye'. The Rawa Fried Chops and Butter Garlic Prawn recipes were a hit as expected, but the high of this tryst with the camera was quite a pleasant surprise!

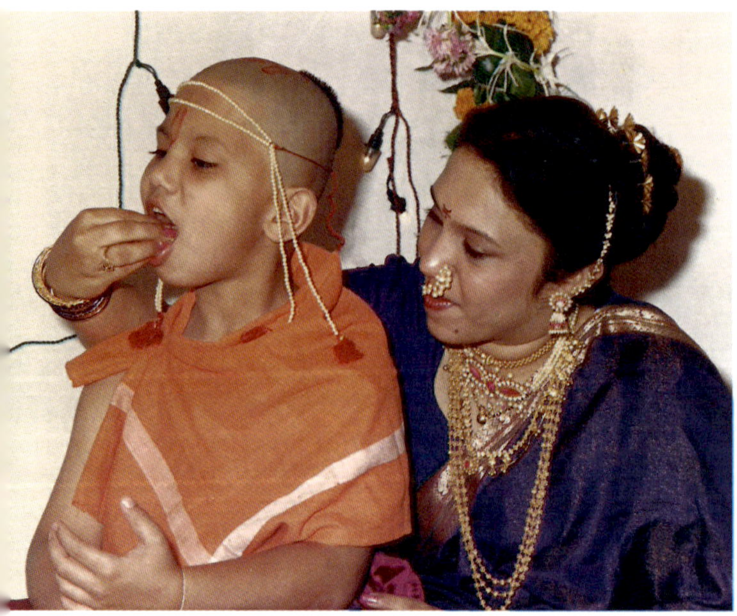

This experience opened a whole new window of opportunity and so after 16 years of working a 9 to 5 job as a paramedic I put down my lab coat and put on a chef's hat and turned my hobby into a passion.

Soon after, I was selected as a contestant for The FoodFood Maha Challenge, a Reality-TV Cooking Competition judged by none other than Chef Sanjeev Kapoor. Interacting with him, the other contestants and judges on that show gave me the right perspective to pursue my passion in the food industry. I'd made the big move from feeding just friends and family to reaching millions of people by sharing

my recipes on ' Sanjeev Kapoor Khazana' and eventually on my own show called My Coastal Kitchen with India Food Network. During this time I did a lot of research to streamline the plethora of recipes I wanted to share with the world. I called my mother for little nuances in the recipes and did trials at home to get the quantities on point contrary to the usual 'andaaz' measurement we follow in India.

This kitchen has always been my safe space - it is where I go if I'm in a good mood and it is where I go to make a bad mood good. It is the tunnel that takes me straight to my husband's heart and keeps me in my son's memories when working in London makes him too homesick! This kitchen is where I relive the good times of travels to Russia and Japan as I recreate food I'd sampled there. This is the kitchen that has witnessed my journey from Varan Bhaat to Biryani, this is where my romance with food truly began - This is Roopa's Kitchen!

मसाला MASALA DOODH

Saffron flavoured milk

This is one of my signature recipes. It became quite famous amongst friends and relatives who visited (and still visit) our home for a Satyanarayan Pooja we have during the month of Shravan. Shravan occurs during monsoon and with that slight nip in the air, masala doodh feels just like a warm hug. Slightly reducing the sweetened milk adds a certain smooth consistency, while dried fruits, saffron and spices add layers of flavour. I like to serve it with 'Prasadacha Sheera' and follow it up with a little nap afterwards.

Ingredients:

- 1 tablespoon cashew nuts
- 1 tablespoon charoli (chronji)
- 1 tablespoon pistachios
- 4-5 almonds
- ½ teaspoon nutmeg powder
- A few saffron strands
- 1 litre milk
- ¼ cup sugar
- 1 tablespoon almonds, blanched, peeled and cut into slivers
- A pinch of green cardamom (elaichi) powder

Method:

Heat the milk in a non-stick pan and bring it to a boil. Reduce the heat and simmer till the milk reduces to three-fourth of the quantity, stirring occasionally.

Place the cashew nuts, charoli, pistachios, almonds, nutmeg powder and saffron strands into a grinder jar and grind to a coarse powder.

Add the sugar and three tablespoons of ground powder in the milk mixture and mix well. Add the almond slivers and green cardamom powder and stir well. Simmer for ten to twelve minutes, stirring occasionally.

Take the milk off the heat and pour into individual serving glasses. Serve hot or chilled.

Preparation Time: 10-15 minutes
Cooking Time: 08-10 minutes
Serves: 4

PAACH POHE

We all have diwali memories involving food - of either making it or eating it! Besides regular diwali faral like chakli, chiwda, karanji, anarsa etc. we also follow the tradition of making 5 types of Pohe for breakfast on diwali mornings. For years I made large batches of this for my son and his school friends who would come home each year after a visit to the nearby Parleshwar temple. Their big breakfast treat on Narak Chaturdashi Day included these 5 types of Pohe namely - Dahi pohe, Haath Churme Pohe, Kande Pohe, Metkut Pohe and Gul Pohe plus a portion of Kala Vatanyachi Usal (spicy black pea curry). Although 5 types of poha might seem monotonous, but trust me, the flavours are wondrous and each one adds a different something to the plate, quite literally.

Ingredients:

1½ cups chilled yogurt

1 cup flattened thick poha (jada poha)

Salt to taste

1 teaspoon sugar

1 green chilli

½ inch ginger

Method:

Place the flattened rice in a strainer and wash thoroughly under running water. Set aside till the water drains out.

Whisk together the yogurt with salt and sugar in a large bowl.

Pound the green chilli and ginger together in a mortar and pestle and mix it with the yogurt.

Squeeze the flattened rice for any excess water and add to the yogurt mixture and mix well. Serve.

DAHI दही POHE

Flattened Rice with Yogurt

Preparation Time: 10-15 minutes
Cooking Time: 0 minutes
Serves: 4 small servings or 2 pax

कांदे KANDE POHE

Flattened Rice with Onion and Potatoes

Ingredients:

2 medium onions (kande), finely sliced

3 cups thick flattened rice (jada poha), washed and drained

3 tablespoons oil

½ teaspoon mustard seeds

1 teaspoon cumin seeds

3 green chillies, roughly chopped

½ teaspoon turmeric powder

¼ teaspoon asafoetida (hing)

1 medium potato, peeled and diced

Salt to taste

1 teaspoon sugar

2 tablespoons chopped fresh coriander

¼ cup grated fresh coconut

Lemon wedge to serve

Method:

Heat the oil in a kadai. Add the mustard seeds, cumin seeds, green chillies, turmeric, asafoetida and onions and fry till they are translucent.

Add the potatoes, salt, one-fourth cup of water and cover and cook till the potatoes are half-cooked.

Add the flattened rice and mix well. Adjust the salt, cover and cook further for three minutes on low heat.

Sprinkle some water if needed, add the sugar and mix. Cover and cook further for two to three minutes or till the potatoes are cooked.

Garnish with coriander leaves and coconut and serve with a lemon wedge.

Preparation Time: 10-15 minutes
Cooking Time: 20-25 minutes
Serves: 4

GUL POHE पोहे

Flattened Rice with Jaggery

Ingredients:

¾ cup grated jaggery

1½ cups thick flattened red rice (jada lal poha)

1 cup grated fresh coconut

½ cup coconut water

½ teaspoon green cardamom powder

A pinch of salt

¼ cup warm ghee

Method:

Place the flattened rice in a bowl and sprinkle coconut water on it till the poha becomes moist. Add the grated fresh coconut, green cardamom powder, salt and jaggery. Mix with hands till well combined.

Drizzle warm ghee and serve.

Preparation Time: 10-15 minutes
Cooking Time: 0 minutes
Serves: 4 small servings or 2 pax

HAATH CHURME पोहे POHE

Flattened rice with Fresh Coconut

Ingredients:

1½ cups thick flattened rice (jada poha)

½ cup coconut water

1 cup grated fresh coconut

Salt to taste

¾ teaspoon asafoetida (hing)

2 green chillies, roughly chopped

Method:

Place the beaten rice in a bowl and sprinkle coconut water on it till the beaten rice is moist.

Add the grated coconut, salt, asafoetida , chillies and mix with your hands till well combined.

Serve immediately.

Preparation Time: 10-15 minutes
Cooking Time: 0 minutes
Serves: 4 small servings or 2 pax

METKUT

मेतकूट POHE

Lightly Spiced Flattened Rice

Ingredients:

1 tablespoon metkut *(pg no 153)*

1 cup thin flattened rice (patla poha)

1 small onion, finely chopped

¼ cup fresh grated coconut

2 tablespoons roasted peanuts

½ teaspoon sugar

Salt to taste

1 tablespoon lemon juice

1 tablespoon ghee

½ teaspoon mustard seeds

½ teaspoon cumin seeds

¼ teaspoon asafoetida (hing)

1 green chilli, roughly chopped

2 tablespoons chopped fresh coriander leaves

Method:

Place the flattened rice in a bowl, add the onion, grated coconut, peanuts, sugar, salt, lemon juice, metkut and mix well.

Heat the ghee in a small tempering pan. Add the mustard seeds, cumin seeds, asafoetida, and green chilli and sauté for a few seconds. Pour this over the flattened rice mixture and mix till well combined.

Garnish with coriander leaves and serve immediately.

Preparation Time: 10-15 minutes
Cooking Time: 0-5 minutes
Serves: 4 small servings or 2 pax

CHUTNEY PAPLET
पापलेट
Stuffed Pomfret

Several communities in India make green masala style fish - from the Parsi Patrani Machi to Bengali Macher Paturi. My version has whole white pomfrets stuffed with a lightly spiced, green mint chutney. Chutney Paplet is definitely a special occasion treat in my home, thanks to all the TLC that goes into making it.

Method:

Marinate the fish with salt, turmeric powder, sambar powder, red chilli powder and ginger-garlic-green chilli paste and mix well. Set aside for ten minutes.

For the chutney, finely grind coconut, mint, coriander, garlic, green chillies, salt, tamarind and a little water in a mixer jar.

Heat the oil in a pan. Add the chutney and sauté for a minute. Add the garam masala powder and sauté till the mixture starts to leave the sides of the pan. Take the pan off the heat and set aside to cool completely.

Heat the sufficient oil in a non-stick shallow pan.

Spread the rice flour on a plate, add the semolina and mix well.

Stuff each fish with the sautéed chutney and tie the fish with a thread to secure it. Coat the stuffed fish with the rice flour mixture and gently place it in the hot oil. Shallow-fry on medium heat till golden brown from both sides. Approx. two to three minutes on each side.

Arrange the shallow fried fish on a serving plate, garnish with onion rings, coriander sprigs and lemon wedges. Serve hot.

Preparation Time: 10 minutes
Cooking Time: 20-25 minutes
Serves: 4

Sautéing the chutney before stuffing ensures to get rid of excess moisture from the chutney.

Ingredients:

2 medium-sized pomfret (paplet), cleaned, slit sideways along the central bone without cutting through

Salt to taste

½ teaspoon turmeric powder

1 teaspoon sambar powder *(pg no. 153)*

½ teaspoon red chilli powder

1 teaspoon ginger-garlic-green chilli paste

Oil for shallow-frying

½ cup rice flour

2 tablespoons semolina (rawa)

Chutney

1 cup grated fresh coconut

½ cup fresh mint leaves

¼ cup fresh coriander leaves

5 garlic cloves

4 green chillies

Salt to taste

1 teaspoon tamarind pulp

1 teaspoon oil

¼ tsp garam masala powder

To garnish

Onions rings as required

A few fresh coriander sprigs

Lemon wedges as required

It is what completes our Naivedya thali at home. Since all the other food items are made without onion and garlic, this tangy, spicy dry-fruit and chilli chutney, along with loncha (pickle), koshimbir (salad) and chutney add zing to the meal. Panchamrut, like the other accompaniments, is always placed on the left side of the Naivedya thali. It's served in small portions but packs a big flavour.

PANCHAMRUT

पंचामृत

Dry Fruit Chutney

Ingredients:

2 tablespoons soaked peanuts

1 tablespoon soaked cashew nuts

2 tablespoons black raisins

2 tablespoons chopped dried dates (kharik)

2 tablespoons grated dried coconut

3 tablespoons oil

2 cloves

½ inch cinnamon stick

1 teaspoon white sesame seeds

½ teaspoon cumin seeds

2 tablespoons peanut powder

1 tablespoon dried coconut slices

½ teaspoon mustard seeds

¼ teaspoon asafoetida (hing)

½ teaspoon turmeric powder

7-8 long light green chillies, roughly chopped

1 medium green capsicum, chopped

1 teaspoon red chilli powder

1 teaspoon goda masala *(pg no 150)*

1 tablespoon tamarind pulp

3 tablespoons grated jaggery

Salt to taste

Method:

Heat one tablespoon of oil in a small pan. Add the cloves, cinnamon, sesame seeds and cumin seeds and sauté till fragrant. Add the grated dried coconut and roast for one to two minutes or till fragrant. Set aside to cool.

Place the cooled roasted spices in a blender jar, add half a cup of water along with peanut powder and blend to a fine paste.

Heat the remaining oil in another pan. Add the mustard seeds and let them crackle. Add the asafoetida, turmeric powder, green chillies, and capsicum and sauté for a minute.

Add the soaked peanuts, cashews, raisins, dried dates and sliced dry coconut slices and sauté for a minute.

Add the red chilli powder, goda masala, salt, and half a cup of water and mix well. Cook on low heat for ten to twelve minutes.

Add the blended coconut paste into the pan, mix and continue to cook for five more minutes.

Add the tamarind pulp and jaggery and mix well. Cook for five minutes or till the mixture thickens. Switch the heat off and transfer into a serving bowl.

Preparation Time: 10-15 hours
Cooking Time: 30-35 minutes

AMBAT BATATA

Tangy Potato Gravy

Every household has a favourite potato dish and in my house, it is Ambat Batata. Made without any onions or garlic, this thick orange gravy laced with chunky potato wedges usually finds place in a Naivedya thali and on several other weekday meals at home. The mildly spiced tangy gravy gets a distinct flavour with a fenugreek seed tempering. It gives tough competition to the typical yellow coloured potato bhaaji or peewli batate chi bhaaji.

Ingredients:

3 large potatoes, peeled and cut into wedges

1 tablespoon tamarind pulp

2 tablespoons oil

½ teaspoon asafoetida (hing)

1 teaspoon fenugreek seeds (methi dana)

½ teaspoon turmeric powder

1½ teaspoons red chilli powder

Salt to taste

½ cup grated fresh coconut

1 teaspoon gram flour (besan)

1 tablespoon grated jaggery

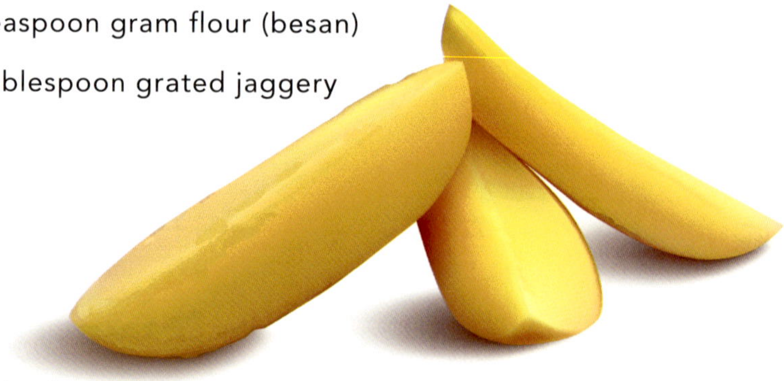

Method:

Heat the oil in a kadai, add the asafoetida, fenugreek seeds and turmeric powder and sauté for a few seconds.

Add the potatoes and sauté on high heat for one minute.

Add the chilli powder, salt and half a cup of water, mix, cover and cook till ¾ done. Approx six to eight minutes.

Finely grind coconut, gram flour, tamarind pulp and half a cup of water.

Add the ground paste to the potato mixture and mix well. Cook on low heat for four to five minutes or till the potatoes are cooked completely.

Increase the heat to medium, add the jaggery, mix and cook for one minute. Reduce the heat to low and cook for another minute. Serve hot.

Preparation Time: 5 minutes
Cooking Time: 10-15 minutes
Serves: 4-5

Ingredients:

750 grams mutton, cut into 2 inch pieces on the bone

2 medium whole onions

1 whole garlic bulb

1 small dried coconut

5 tablespoons oil

1 teaspoon coriander seeds

½ teaspoon cumin seeds

1-inch cinnamon stick

6 cloves

8 black peppercorns

½ teaspoon poppy seeds

2 green cardamoms

8-10 dried red chillies

Salt to taste

1 tablespoon ginger-garlic-green chilli paste

1 medium onion, finely chopped

1 tablespoon finely chopped garlic

2 tablespoons tamarind pulp

Bhakris or steamed rice to serve

Method:

Roast the whole onions and whole garlic bulb on a flame till they appear black. Allow it to cool slightly, peel and cut into big pieces. Set aside.

Roast the dried coconut on a flame, till it appears brown. Allow it to cool, break into small pieces and set aside.

Heat two tablespoons oil, add the coriander seeds, cumin seeds, cinnamon stick, cloves, black peppercorns, poppy seeds, cardamoms and dried red chillies and roast for a minute. Allow it to cool and transfer into a mixer jar. Add the roasted garlic, onion, dried coconut and half a cup of water and grind to a fine thick paste.

To the mutton, add the salt and ginger-garlic-green chilli paste and mix well. Set aside to marinate for ten minutes.

Heat the remaining oil in another pan, add the chopped onion and garlic and sauté till they go brown. Add the marinated mutton and sauté on high heat for a minute. Add half a cup of water, cover and cook on low heat for thirty to thirty-five minutes or till the mutton is three-fourth done. Add water as required to adjust consistency.

Add the ground paste and half a cup of water, mix, cover and cook further for ten minutes on low heat.

Add the tamarind pulp and mix well. Add the water if needed to adjust the consistency. It should form a thick gravy. Continue to cook for five minutes.

Serve with bhakri or steamed rice.

KAALE MUTTON

Roasted spiced Mutton Masala

One of my favourite mutton preparations, Kaale Mutton is something that I happened to try once at a restaurant in Nashik called Divtya Budlya and the flavours stayed with me so I decided to recreate it in my kitchen. 'Kaala' which means black in Marathi. While the name is a bit of a giveaway, the flavours are a complete surprise in a good way. Besides charred onions, coconut and garlic pods, tamarind contributes significantly to the deep, dark colour and wonderful taste of this unique curry.

Preparation Time: 10-15 minutes
Cooking Time: 1 hour
Serves: 4

कोंबडी
KOMBDI VADE

Malvani Chicken Curry with fried Multigrain Puri

Ingredients:

- 750 grams chicken, curry cut
- 1 tablespoon ginger-garlic-green chilli paste
- 1 tablespoon Malvani Masala (pg no 152)
- 1 teaspoon red chilli powder
- ½ teaspoon turmeric powder
- Salt to taste
- 4 tablespoons oil
- 3 medium onions, finely chopped
- 1 medium tomato, finely chopped
- 1 teaspoon garam masala powder
- 1 teaspoon coriander seeds
- 1 teaspoon fennel seeds (saunf)
- 1 teaspoon white sesame seeds
- 1 star anise
- ½ inch cinnamon stick
- 3-4 cloves
- 3-4 black peppercorns
- ¼ cup grated fresh coconut
- ¼ cup grated dried coconut
- 2-3 tablespoons chopped fresh coriander leaves

Method:

Combine the chicken with ginger-garlic-chilli paste, Malvani masala, red chilli powder, turmeric powder and salt. Mix well and set aside to marinate for five to ten minutes.

Heat three tablespoons of oil in a pan. Add half the onions and sauté till golden. Add the tomato, mix and cook till soft.

Add the marinated chicken and sauté on high heat for two to three minutes.

Add the garam masala powder and mix well.

Add one cup of water, stir to mix, cover and cook for ten minutes on medium heat.

Heat the remaining oil in another pan. Add the coriander seeds, fennel seeds and sesame seeds and let them crackle.

Add the star anise, cinnamon, cloves and peppercorns and sauté till fragrant.

Add the remaining onions and sauté till golden.

Add the fresh coconut and mix. Cook till golden. Add the dried coconut and mix till it turns golden. Take the pan off the heat and set aside to cool. Transfer to a mixer jar, add half a cup of water and grind to a fine paste.

Add the ground paste to the chicken mixture and mix well. Cover and cook for ten minutes on low heat.

Add the coriander leaves and mix well.

Take the pan off the heat and serve hot with vade (pg no 143).

Preparation Time: 15-20 minutes
Cooking Time: 40-45 minutes
Serves: 4-6

A staple from the Malvan region, Kombdi Vade is made for occasions, celebrations and grand Sunday lunches. It is a must-have in post-wedding rituals in our village, like it is for meat lovers at every Malvani restaurant. A dish that I have on the menu when I intend to introduce someone to non-vegetarian Maharashtrian cuisine which includes my son Gaurang's friends from different parts of the world.

मटण

MUTTON

Semolina Coated Mutton Chops

CHOPS RAWA FRY

The best things in life are the result of an odd innovation and this Mutton Chops Rawa Fry is a great example of that. I created this dish when I decided to treat a wonderful rack of lamb chops the same way that I would treat a fresh batch of fish and rawa fry them. The result is this crisp, succulent, meaty treat which has somewhat become a star attraction at every party I host. My friends and family dig into these with a vengeance, so I have to always make a large batch and that works out just fine because it's a recipe that I truly enjoy making!

Ingredients:

8-10 mutton chops

½ cup fine semolina (barik rawa)

½ cup chopped fresh coriander leaves

4-5 green chillies, roughly chopped

½ inch ginger

6-7 garlic cloves

Salt to taste

1 tablespoon Kolhapuri Kanda Lasoon Masala *(pg no 151)*

½ teaspoon turmeric powder

1 teaspoon red chilli powder

1 tablespoon oil

2 eggs

Oil for deep-frying

Method:

Grind together the coriander leaves, green chillies, ginger, garlic and a little water, into a fine paste.

To the mutton, add the ground paste, salt, Kolhapuri Kanda Lasoon Masala, turmeric powder and red chilli powder. Mix well and set aside to marinate for five to ten minutes.

Heat the oil in a pressure cooker. Add the mutton chops along with the marinade and sauté for one minute.

Add half a cup of water and stir to mix. Cover and pressure cook on high heat for one whistle. Reduce the heat to low and continue to cook for six to eight minutes. Remove from heat and set aside to cool.

Heat sufficient oil in a kadai.

Whisk the eggs in a bowl. Spread the semolina on a plate.

Dip chops one by one in the eggs and coat well with semolina. Dust off the excess.

Heat the oil in a kadhai. Slide in the chops a few at a time in the hot oil and deep-fry till golden and crisp. Drain on absorbent paper. Serve hot.

Preparation Time: 20-25 minutes
Cooking Time: 25-30 minutes
Serves: 4-5

CKP MUTTON

Traditional Mutton Curry

Chandraseniya Kayastha Prabhu or CKP is a community from the Konkan region and while there are many similarities in the cooking styles with the GSB community, unlike our traditional recipes theirs include significant amounts of ginger, garlic and spices. This recipe was shared with me by one of my closest friends, Jyotsna Kirpekar, who belongs to the CKP community. Having it on the menu while hosting friends at home always brings a few compliments my way!

Ingredients:

750 grams mutton on the bone, cut into 1½-inch pieces

1 medium onion, chopped

1 tablespoon coriander seeds

2 teaspoons fennel seeds (saunf)

1-inch ginger

2 tbsps chopped fresh coriander leaves + for garnish

4-6 garlic cloves

4-5 peppercorns

2-3 green chillies

½ inch cinnamon stick

Salt to taste

1 teaspoon asafoetida (hing)

2 teaspoons red chilli powder

3 tablespoons oil

2 medium onions, sliced

1½ teaspoons garam masala powder

1 cup coconut milk

Method:

For the marinade, add the chopped onion to a mixer jar. Add the coriander seeds, fennel seeds, ginger, coriander leaves, garlic, green chillies, peppercorns, cinnamon, and sufficient water and grind to a fine paste.

Take the mutton in a large bowl, add the salt, half a teaspoon of asafoetida, one teaspoon red chilli powder and the ground paste and mix well. Add one tablespoon of oil and set aside to marinate for ten to fifteen minutes.

Heat the remaining oil in a pan, add the remaining asafoetida and sliced onion and sauté till it turns light brown.

Add the mutton and sauté on high heat for four to five minutes. Add the remaining red chilli powder and garam masala powder and mix well.

Add two cups of water and bring to a boil. Cover and cook on low heat, stirring occasionally, for fifty to fifty-five minutes or till the mutton is almost cooked.

Add the coconut milk and mix well. Bring to a gentle boil, reduce the heat to low and cook for five minutes.

Garnish with coriander leaves and serve hot.

Preparation Time: 15-20 minutes
Cooking Time: 1-1.5 hours
Serves: 4-6

MORI MUTTON

Baby Shark Masala

Shakespeare rightly said, what's in a name!? And in the case of this dish, he was right. While the name of this curry may be misleading, the flavour profile that leads you to food heaven surely isn't. Mori or baby shark is cooked in a masala that is traditionally used to prepare mutton. It works beautifully because of the firm texture of the fish. Shark is not the most popular choice of seafood, but when made, it's quite a feast!

Preparation Time: 10-15 hours
Cooking Time: 20-25 minutes
Serves: 4-5

Ingredients:

1 medium-sized baby shark (mori), skinned, cleaned and cut into medium-sized pieces

1 tablespoon ginger-garlic paste

½ teaspoon turmeric powder

1 teaspoon red chilli powder

1 teaspoon garam masala powder

Salt to taste

2 medium onions, finely chopped

3 tablespoons oil

4 black peppercorns

4 cloves

1-inch cinnamon stick

1 teaspoon coriander seeds

1 teaspoon poppy seeds

5 garlic cloves

½ cup grated fresh coconut

1 tablespoon tamarind pulp

Method:

To the fish, add the ginger-garlic paste, turmeric, red chilli powder, garam masala powder, salt, and sprinkle one finely chopped onion and rub the masala well on the fish and set aside to marinate for five minutes.

Heat one tablespoon of oil in a shallow pan. Add the peppercorns, cloves, cinnamon, coriander seeds, poppy seeds and garlic and sauté well. Add half of the remaining finely chopped onion and sauté till brown.

Add the grated coconut and fry on low heat for five minutes or till it turns golden brown. Take the pan off the heat and allow it to cool. Transfer into a mixer jar and grind to a fine paste using around two or three tablespoons of water.

Heat the remaining oil in a kadai. Add the remaining onion and sauté for two minutes. Add the marinated fish and sauté on high heat for one minute.

Add half a cup of water, mix and cook on low heat for five minutes. Add the ground masala, and tamarind pulp. Add the water to adjust the consistency (it should be a thick gravy) and mix well. Continue to cook for five minutes.

Serve hot.

STUFFED CRABS

The first time that I had this magnificent dish was when my sister–in-law Anju's mom, whom we fondly called Neemu aaji made it. One morsel on my tongue and my mind was blown and I just had to recreate it in my kitchen. After getting the recipe from her, I tried it a couple of times before finally perfecting it. The process is a little tedious but very rewarding and you have to be on the list of my favourite people for me to make it for you!

Ingredients:

4 medium-sized whole crabs

2 tablespoons butter

½ teaspoon asafoetida (hing)

½ cup finely chopped onions

¼ teaspoon nutmeg powder

1 tablespoon minced garlic

3 green chillies, finely chopped

¾ teaspoon black pepper powder

¼ cup fresh coriander chopped finely

1 tablespoon lemon juice

4 tablespoons grated processed cheese

1 tablespoon refined flour

½ cup milk

1 teaspoon Tabasco sauce

4 tablespoons breadcrumbs

Salt to taste

Method:

Boil the crabs till they turn orange or for five to ten minutes. Then shell them carefully, wash well and set the outer shells aside.The meat from the claws and abdomen of the 4 crabs should be about 3 cups.

Heat a pan, add the butter, asafoetida, onions, garlic, chillies, and sauté for a minute.

Add the pepper powder, nutmeg powder, salt. Mix well and saute for one minute.

Add the crab meat, mix gently for a minute. Sprinkle maida, add the milk and mix well.

Add the fresh coriander, lemon juice and tabasco sauce, mix and put off the flame.

Once cool, stuff the 4 shells of the crabs with cooked crab meat. Sprinkle cheese, layer with bread crumbs and bake in pre-heated oven at 180°C for five minutes or till cheese melts. Serve.

Best crabs are available during the new moon day.

Preparation Time: 45-50 hours
Cooking Time: 10-15 minutes
Serves: 4

I consider this my signature dish. This recipe is a very important pit stop in my food journey. As someone who couldn't make simple dal chawal without creating a furore to being able to pull off making three kilos of this magnificent biryani with ease. Why! I can even take a nap in between, while the aromas of this dum biryani fill my house. Making a biryani seems like a daunting task to most and I was no different, but getting this one right with ease will give you the push you need to overcome those inhibitions. It sure worked for me. While the melange of flavours created by fragrant rice, succulent meat and select spices are much appreciated, it is the soft mushy potatoes that are the star of this dish in my house. Skipping them is just not an option.

KACHCHE GOSHT KI DUM BIRYANI

Ingredients:

1 kg mutton, cut into bite-size pieces on the bone

½ kg Basmati rice, soaked for 20 minutes

1 tablespoon ginger-garlic-green chilli paste

1½ cups yogurt

Salt to taste

4-5 green cardamoms

1 star anise

1 teaspoon cumin seeds

1 mace blade

1-inch cinnamon stick

½ teaspoon turmeric powder

1½ teaspoons red chilli powder

4 cloves

1 teaspoon caraway seeds (shahi jeera)

5 black peppercorns

½ teaspoon nutmeg powder

1 teaspoon garam masala powder

Juice of 1 lemon

3 medium potatoes, halved

2 bay leaves

2 black cardamoms

4 tablespoons ghee + for drizzling

1½ cups browned onion + for garnishing

1 teaspoon saffron strands, soaked in 1-2 tablespoons warm water

Wheat flour dough for sealing

Method:

Marinate the mutton with ginger-garlic-green chilli paste, yogurt, salt, three green cardamoms, star anise, cumin seeds, mace, cinnamon, turmeric powder, red chilli powder, cloves, caraway seeds, black peppercorns, nutmeg powder, garam masala powder and lemon juice and mix well. Add the potatoes and mix again and set aside for thirty minutes.

Meanwhile, boil sufficient water in a deep pan. Add the salt, bay leaves, remaining green cardamoms, black cardamom and rice and mix well. Cook for one minute and drain the first half of the rice and set aside.

Continue to cook further for two minutes. Drain and set aside.

Grease the bottom of a handi with ghee. Place the marinated mutton and potatoes in the handi and spread evenly.

Spread the browned onion and drizzle a little ghee on top. Spread the first half of the drained rice followed by the remaining rice and spread it evenly. Drizzle some more ghee on it and around the edges as well.

Add the soaked saffron on top and tightly cover the handi with aluminium foil. Place the lid on top, seal the edges with dough.

Place the handi on heat and cook on high heat for six to eight minutes. Reduce the heat to low, place the handi on a non-stick tawa and cook under dum for about forty-five minutes. Remove the dough and open the lid.

Serve hot garnished with browned onions.

Preparation Time: 25-30 minutes
Cooking Time: 1-1.5 hours
Serves: 6-8

MASALE BHAAT

Vegetable Pulao

Ingredients:

1½ cups mixed vegetables (like diced brinjal, carrot, small cauliflower florets, green peas, lengthwise quartered ivy gourds)

2 cups short-grain rice, washed and drained

3 tablespoons oil

4 black peppercorns

2 cloves

1-inch cinnamon stick

1 bay leaf

½ teaspoon mustard seeds

½ teaspoon cumin seeds

½ teaspoon asafoetida (hing)

½ teaspoon turmeric powder

Few curry leaves

2 green chillies, slit

1 teaspoon red chilli powder

1 teaspoon goda masala *(pg no. 150)*

Salt to taste

1 tablespoon grated jaggery

4 -5 kokum petals

10-15 cashew nuts, soaked in 1 cup water

Fresh grated coconut for garnish

Chopped fresh coriander leaves for garnish

The second of the two rice dishes served in a Pangat, which is a seated full-course Maharashtrian community meal - Masale Bhaat is fancier and more flavourful than its first cousin Varan Bhaat. While most people might make it with just brinjal and ivy gourd, at the Patki household, Masale Bhaat is loaded with veggies! The use of goda masala adds a special flavour that cannot be replicated with regular powdered spices. In fact no onion or garlic is used either. So even though it is called such, Masale Bhaat is more about flavour than spice.

Method:

Heat the oil, add the black peppercorns, cloves, cinnamon stick, bay leaf, mustard seeds, cumin seeds, asafoetida, turmeric powder, curry leaves and green chillies and sauté for few seconds.

Add the rice and sauté for two minutes. Add the mixed vegetables, red chilli powder, goda masala and salt and sauté for a minute.

Add four cups of boiling water, cover and cook for eight minutes or till the rice and vegetables are almost done.

Add the jaggery and kokum petals, soaked cashew nuts, mix together, cover and cook for two minutes or till completely cooked.

Garnish with coconut and coriander leaves. Serve hot.

Preparation Time: 10-15 minutes
Cooking Time: 15-20 minutes
Serves: 6-8

While I prefer to make this recipe with Ambe Mohar rice or Indrayani rice, you can use any short grain rice of your choice.

Kombdi Vade are like the 'perfect couple' in the coastal kitchen. While the chicken curry tends to be the hero upfront, it is the vade that is the secret to the success and popularity of this dish. The fact that they are deep-fried and a little time consuming to make have resulted in them becoming kind of obsolete in the home kitchen. Something that I think is quite silly, because they are still healthier than a lot of junk food you would normally mindlessly indulge in.

Ingredients:

2 cups vada flour

1 tablespoon oil + for deep-frying

Salt to taste

1 tablespoon tamarind pulp

A pinch of turmeric powder

Method:

For the vada dough, heat one tablespoon of oil in a tempering pan.

Combine the vada flour, salt, tamarind pulp, turmeric powder and hot oil in a bowl. Knead into a soft dough using sufficient water, cover and set aside for thirty to forty-five minutes.

Divide the dough into twelve to fourteen equal portions and shape each portion into a small ball.

Apply a little water on a zip-lock bag, place a ball on it and pat to make a small disc. Make a small hole in the centre. This is a vada. Similarly, make the remaining vades.

Heat sufficient oil in a kadai. Slide in the vades one at a time into the hot oil and deep fry till golden brown and puffed up. Drain on absorbent paper. Serve.

Multigrain Puri VADE

For the vada flour, wash 250 grams rice thoroughly and let it dry over a muslin cloth for 5-6 hours under the sun. Lightly dry-roast 50 grams each of whole wheat, split skinless black gram (dhuli urad dal), Bengal gram (chana dal), sorghum (jowar), ½ tablespoon fenugreek seeds (methi dana), 1 tablespoon coriander seeds, 1 tablespoon cumin seeds, 1 tablespoon fennel seeds (saunf) individually and allow it to cool slightly. Finely grind all the roasted mixture along with the dried rice. Sift the flour and grind the residue to a fine powder. Store into an airtight container and it can stay for upto 4 months. Readymade vada flour is also available in the stores.

Preparation Time: 45-50 minutes
Cooking Time: 10-15 minutes
Serves: 4-5

वरण

Plain Dal VARAN

The first good meal and one of the most precious memories I have in my life is of making Varan Bhaat for the first time. It was what I cooked for Gaurang when he turned 5 months and I had to feed him his first solid meal. My maternal instincts kicked in and I just dived headfirst into the kitchen and set out to make that perfect meal of Varan Bhaat for my dear son. The passion and love that went into making it was far more than my pasta-noodle experiments in the kitchen as a new bride. Getting this simple recipe just perfect meant so much more than cooking any other meal and I think that's where my romance with cooking began.

Varan Bhaat, toop (ghee) and limbu (lemon) is the original complete meal packed with carbohydrates, fats, protein, vitamins and plenty of flavours. According to my husband, Varan which is served in a pangat or traditional Maharashtrian feast is the best and can never be replicated at home because the flavour that comes through when cooked in large quantities for hours is unique.

Varan Bhaat is a dish that every member of a Maharashtrian household, irrespective of age and taste preferences will mutually agree is a favourite.

Ingredients:

1 cup split pigeon peas (tur dal), washed, soaked for 5-10 minutes and drained

¼ teaspoon turmeric powder

½ teaspoon asafoetida (hing)

¼ teaspoon coarsely crushed cumin seeds

Salt to taste

Steamed rice to serve

Ghee to serve

Method:

Put the split pigeon peas in a pressure cooker, add double the quantity of water and cook on high heat till one whistle and then cook under pressure on low heat for five to six minutes. Switch off the heat.

Open the cooker only once the pressure has settled completely. Transfer the cooked dal to a deep pan. Add the turmeric powder, asafoetida, cumin seeds, salt, and one cup of hot water and mix well. Cook on low heat for four to five minutes.

Serve hot with steamed rice along with a dollop of ghee.

Preparation Time: 10 minutes
Cooking Time: 20-25 minutes
Serves: 4-5

MASOORICHI GODI SHAAK

Whole Red Lentil Curry

For Maharashtrians, the most common way to cook pulses is as an ussal, but Masoorichi Godi Shaak is something quite different. It is a thin coconut-based curry and is best eaten with steamed rice. Simple, flavourful and tangy, the mention of 'godi' which means sweet in Marathi can be quite misleading because this curry is not sweet at all.

Ingredients:

1½ cups whole red lentils (akha masoor), soaked and sprouted

1 medium onion, chopped

½ cup grated fresh coconut

1 teaspoon cumin seeds

1½ teaspoons red chilli powder

½ teaspoon turmeric powder

1 teaspoon garam masala powder

Salt to taste

1 teaspoon tamarind pulp

1 tablespoon oil

1½ tablespoons chopped garlic

Method:

Combine the lentils, onion and one cup of water in a deep pan. Cover and cook for ten minutes.

Grind together the coconut, cumin seeds with one-fourth cup of water, to a smooth paste.

Add the red chilli powder, turmeric powder, garam masala powder and salt to the cooking lentils and mix well.

Add half a cup of water, stir, cover and cook for two minutes or till the lentils go soft. Add the tamarind pulp and ground paste, mix well and simmer for two minutes.

Heat the oil in a small pan. Add the garlic and sauté till it turns golden brown.

Add the sautéed garlic to the lentil mixture and cover the pan and take off the heat. Serve hot.

Preparation Time: 2 hours for soaking and 8 hours for sprouting
Cooking Time: 15-20 minutes
Serves: 4-6

MANGANA

Bengal Gram Kheer

There are kheers and then there is Mangana, I promise you this one is a notch above the usual rice or vermicelli kheers you might have tried. Chana dal and mushy sago pearls create brilliant contrast in texture while the caramelised jaggery, pure ghee and coconut milk add layers of flavour. Make sure you make a larger batch than expected because people are always going to come back asking for another helping of Mangana. It is the perfect way to end things on a sweet note.

Ingredients:

½ cup split Bengal gram (chana dal), soaked for 4 hours

¼ cup nylon sago (sabudana), soaked for 4 hours

3 tablespoons small pieces of fresh coconut

1 cup grated jaggery

2 tablespoons broken cashew nuts

A pinch of salt

1 cup thin coconut milk

1 tablespoon rice flour

1 cup thick coconut milk

1 teaspoon green cardamom powder

Method:

Boil two cups of water in a deep pan. Add the split Bengal gram, nylon sago, and coconut and mix well. Cover and cook on low heat for fifteen minutes.

Add the jaggery, cashew nuts, and salt and mix well. Cook further for three minutes.

Combine the thin coconut milk and the rice flour mix well. Add this mixture to the pan and mix well. Continue to cook for two minutes.

Add the thick coconut milk, and green cardamom powder and mix till well combined. Cook on low heat for five minutes or till the dal becomes completely soft and forms a homogenous mixture.

Serve hot.

In case you cannot find nylon sago you can substitute it with ¼ cup sago and soak it for 2 hours.

Preparation Time: 4 hours
Cooking Time: 25-30 minutes
Serves: 4

MASALA

मसाला

GODA MASALA

Ingredients:

4 cups coriander seeds

3 dried red chillies

1 cup grated dried coconut

½ cup white sesame seeds (safed til)

½ cup black sesame seeds (kala til)

¼ cup cumin seeds (jeera)

4-5 teaspoons black cumin seeds (kala jeera)

A small piece of stone flower (dagad phool)

1 tablespoon tiny pieces of cinnamon stick

1 star anise

3-4 cloves

1 black cardamom (seeds only)

2 teaspoons asafoetida (hing)

1 teaspoon turmeric powder

½ teaspoon salt

1 tablespoon oil

Method:

Individually roast the coriander seeds, dried red chillies, and dried coconut with a little oil on low flame till they turn golden and fragrant. Transfer to a large plate and allow it to cool.

Roast the white sesame seeds, black sesame seeds, cumin seeds, black cumin seeds, stone flower, cinnamon, star anise, cloves, and black cardamom with a little oil on low flame till fragrant. Transfer on to the same plate and allow it to cool.

Transfer the roasted spices into a grinder jar, add the asafoetida, turmeric powder, and salt and grind to a fine powder.

Store in an airtight container and use as required.

Preparation Time: 0-5 minutes
Cooking Time: 10-15 minutes
Serves: 300 grams

This spice mix can stay for up to 6 months.

KOLHAPURI KANDA LASOON MASALA

Ingredients:

200 grams byadgi dried red chillies (mirchi)

200 grams Kashmiri dried red chillies (mirchi)

100 grams dried lavangi chillies (mirchi)

250 ml oil + for drizzling

100 grams garlic

¼ kilogram onion, sliced

1 cup chopped fresh coriander leaves

¼ kilogram grated dried coconut

125 grams coriander seeds (dhania)

50 grams cumin seeds (jeera)

25 grams poppy seeds (khas khas)

10 bay leaves

25 grams black peppercorns

25 grams dried whole turmeric

1 nutmeg, broken into small pieces

5 grams cloves

15 grams cinnamon

1 piece mace blade (javitri)

1 tablespoon caraway seeds (shahi jeera)

10 star anise

1 tablespoon fennel seeds (saunf)

1 tablespoon white sesame seeds

1 tablespoon mustard seeds

1 tablespoon fenugreek seeds (methi dana)

1 tablespoon green cardamoms

½ piece of compound asafoetida (hing)

5 pieces cobra saffron (naag kesar)

10 stone flower (dagad phool)

5 pieces tirphal

¼ kilogram sea salt

Method:

Snip the stems of the dried red chillies.

Dry all the dried red chillies in the sunlight for eight to ten hours or till sunset.

Place the garlic pods and onions on large plates individually and drizzle fifty ml oil in each. Similarly, spread coriander leaves and dried coconut on individual plates and drizzle little oil on each. Allow these to dry in the sunlight for eight to ten hours or till sunset.

Heat remaining oil in a large kadai, roast the whole spices in the sequence starting from coriander seeds to tirphal till they turn golden and fragrant. Add the dried red chillies, and dried coconut and roast for a few seconds. Add the dried onion slices and dried garlic pods and roast for a few seconds. Lastly, add the dried coriander leaves and mix well. Allow the mixture to cool completely.

Add the sea salt and this mixture is ready to be ground to a powder.

Store refrigerated in an airtight container and use as required.

If using a household grinder then ensure to grind in small batches and in intervals. The masala should be refrigerated at all times. It can be stored for 1 year.

Preparation Time: 10-12 hours
Cooking Time: 15-20 minutes
Serves: 1.5 kgs

MALVANI MASALA

Ingredients:

15 dried red chillies

2 tablespoons coriander seeds

½ teaspoon mustard seeds

2 teaspoons fennel seeds (saunf)

1 teaspoon caraway seeds (shahi jeera)

4 inch cinnamon stick, broken into pieces

1 star anise

A small piece of stone flower (dagad phool)

1 mace blade

5 cloves

2 black cardamoms

8 black peppercorns

1 teaspoon nutmeg powder

½ teaspoon turmeric powder

¼ teaspoon asafoetida (hing)

Method:

Dry-roast dried red chillies for a minute. Set aside to cool.

Dry-roast the coriander seeds, mustard seeds, fennel seeds, caraway seeds, cinnamon, star anise, stone flower, mace blade, cloves, black cardamoms, and black peppercorns till fragrant.
Set aside to cool.

Grind the roasted spices along with the dried red chillies, nutmeg powder, turmeric powder, and asafoetida to a fine powder.

Preparation Time: 15-20 minutes
Cooking Time: 5-10 minutes
Serves: 100 grams

METKUT

Ingredients:

½ cup split Bengal gram (chana dal)

¼ cup rice

3 tablespoons split skinless black gram (dhuli urad dal)

1 tablespoon coriander seeds

1 teaspoon cumin seeds

1 tablespoon red chilli powder

1 teaspoon turmeric powder

Method:

Dry-roast split Bengal gram, rice, split skinless black gram, coriander seeds and cumin seeds individually till they turn fragrant. Allow it to cool slightly.

Transfer the roasted mixture to a blender jar, add the red chilli powder and turmeric powder and grind to a fine powder. Store in an airtight container and use as required.

We usually make a small batch of Metkut so that the flavour and fragrance are retained.

Preparation Time: 10-15 hours Cooking Time: 15-20 minutes Serves: 4

SAMBAR MASALA

Ingredients:

500 grams coriander seeds

125 grams dried byadgi red chillies

25 grams dried whole turmeric

125 grams black peppercorns

50 grams fenugreek seeds (methi dana)

75 grams split skinless black gram (dhuli urad dal)

Method:

Individually dry-roast coriander seeds, dried red chillies, dried whole turmeric, black peppercorns, fenugreek seeds, and split skinless black gram till golden and fragrant. Allow it to cool slightly.

Transfer the roasted mixture into a good grinder jar and grind to a fine powder.

Store in an airtight container and use as required.

Preparation Time: 20-25 hours
Cooking Time: 10-15 minutes
Serves: 800-900 grams

SUNDAY MASALA

Ingredients:

15 grams coriander seeds

10 dried red chillies

5 grams cinnamon sticks

5 grams caraway seeds (shahi jeera)

5 grams black peppercorns

5 grams fennel seeds (saunf)

1 stone flower (dagad phool)

1 gram cloves

10 grams grated dried coconut

5 grams dried ginger powder (saunth)

1 teaspoon asafoetida (hing)

Method:

Individually dry-roast coriander seeds, dried red chillies, cinnamon sticks, caraway seeds, black peppercorns, fennel seeds, stone flower, cloves and coconut till they turn golden and fragrant. Allow it to cool.

Transfer the roasted mixture into a grinder jar along with dried ginger powder and asafoetida and grind to a fine powder.

Store in an airtight container and use as required.

Preparation Time: 10-15 minutes
Cooking Time: 5-10 minutes
Serves: 50-60 grams

ACKNOWLEDGEMENTS

My darling son Gaurang for being my perfect critic and getting the best out of me as a mother, cook and human being.

My sister Sonal and my sisters-in-law Anjali and Ranjana for always sticking around - in the good times and the bad!

My nephews Yash, Sahil, Akash and Rishabh and nieces Janhavi and Rishika for being the guinea pigs who willingly taste-test all my kitchen experiments.

Drs. Meena and Ram Prabhoo – for making me dream big and achieve them.

Chef Sanjeev Kapoor and Alyona Kapoor for being the best mentors. I'm also grateful and humbled that Chef Kapoor, an inspiration for anybody to achieve their dreams in the world of food, agreed to write the foreword in my first ever cookbook.

Chef Ranveer & Pallavi Brar, Chef Manoj Vasaikar & Kunal Vijaykar for reviewing my food over the years and now my book with an earnesty that's rare to find these days.

My 4 am friends in life and during the creation of 'My Romance with Food' – Dr. Anita Patel, Dr. Indumati Gopinathan, Dr. Anil Bardoo and Dr. Renuka Bardoo.
I must add that the credit for the title goes to Dr. Anita Patel.

Behind every strong woman is another bunch of strong women to boost her confidence! For me this gang is my friends from when I lived in Nahar Amrit Shakti - Shreya bhabhi, Aneeta, Mona, Sangeeta, Neelam and Reena. My girls, who have always shown faith in my cooking skills and me.

Kunal Vijaykar for guiding me throughout. Whether it was sharing his mother's treasured recipes with me or guiding me with his valuable suggestions whenever I found myself at a crossroad.

Rushina M Ghildiyal, Saloni & Sameer Malkani, Krush Dalal, Dr. P. P. Rao, Kalyan Karmakar the Food Legends of Mumbai Scene, who made me part of the close knit community of food bloggers, home chefs and industry stalwarts in Mumbai, the country and beyond.

My team of ladies that have treated my book like their own and worked on it with me. Nisha Dingra for food photography, Devaki Bavkar for artwork, Sonica Sunderram for content and last but not the least Anupa Das who conceived the book with me, putting up with the innumerable questions, changes and even some of my whims and fancies!

Special thanks to Sachin Bavkar, the odd man out.

Dr. Preetha Nilesh for her insight on GSB history.

How can I forget my Khavayye doctor friends – Pankaj, Rajeev and Anagha for all the good times.

My front line warriors at home - Sharda, Maya and Dilip.

Mr. Harsha Bhatkal and Popular Prakashan team.

Dr. Sanjay Nabar - My backbone, soul mate, the ying to my yang, the calm to my chaos and definitely my better half!

Besides the names mentioned there are tons of people who have helped me become what I am - you know who you are and how grateful I am for your presence in my life!

GLOSSARY

Items of Prepared Food	
Aamboli	Savoury pancake
Ambedal	Bengal Gram Salad
Ambushi	Dried Raw Mango Chunks
Amti	Curry
Bhakri	Flat Bread
Dhodak	Baked Fish Preparation
Kaapa	Fritters
Kalwan	Gravy / Curry
Kheer	Sweetened Gruel
Laadoo	Indian Spherical Sweet
Lonche	Pickle
Metkut	Spiced Dal Powder
Patoli	stuffed coconut crepe
Poley	Pancake
Prasadacha Sheera	Religious Food Offerings
Rassa	Thin Gravy
Toi	Watery Dal preparation
Ukdiche Modak	Steamed Sweet Dumplings

Common Ingredients used in Kitchen	
Aamsul / Sol	Kokum Petal
Alambi	Mushroom
Alsande	Cow Peas
Alu	Colocasia
Ambadi	Sorrel Leaves
Ananas	Pineapple
Anda	Egg
Bangda	Mackerel
Besan	Gram Flour
Bombil	Bombay Duck- Fish
Byadgi Chilli	Type of Red Dry Chilli
Chana Dal	Bengal Gram
Dagadphool	Stone Flower
Dhana	Coriander Seeds
Fanas	Jackfruit
Ghota	Wild Ripe Mangoes
Gul	Jaggery
Hing	Asafoetida
Kabuli Chana	Chick Peas
Kachche Gosht	Raw tender Goat Meat
Kairi	Raw Mango
Kaju	Cashew Nut
Kakdi	Cucumber
Kala Chana	Back Chick Peas

Kala Vatana	Black Peas
Kalva	Oysters
Kande	Onions
Keli	Plantains
Kelphul	Banana Flower
Kolam Rice	Fragrant Mediun Grain Rice
Kolambi	Prawns
Kombdi	Chicken
Kulith	Horse Gram
Limbu	Lemon
Maida	Refined Flour
Masoor	Red Lentil
Matki	Dew Beans
Mayaloo	Malabar Spinach
Methi Dana	Fenugreek Seeds
Mori	Baby Shark
Naagkeshar	Cobra Saffron
Neer Fanas	Bread Fruit
Poha	Flattened Rice
Ratamba	Kokum fruit
Rawas	Indian Salmon
Red Chowli	Haricot Beans
Sandge	Dried Dal Dumplings
Shevgasheng	Drum Stick
Sungta	Shrimps
Tirphal	Type of Sichuan Peppercorn
Tisrya	Clams
Tondli	Ivy Gourd
Toop	Ghee
Turdal	Pigeon Peas
Urad Dal	Black Gram
Usaacha Ras	Sugarcane Juice
Val	Field Beans
Varan	Plain Dal
Vatana	Green Peas
Xepda Mirsang Chilli	Local Red Dry Chilli

Terms used in this Book

Bidacha Tawa	Cast Iron Griddle
Fodni	Tempering
Haat Churme	Hand Mixed
Juggad	Make-shift
Kaale	Black
Kadai	Culdron
Khanawal	Eating House
Paach	Five
Pandhara	White
Pangat	People sitting in a row to eat
Sukke	Dry
Tambada	Fiery Red
Thali	Full Meal Plate
Tikhat	Spicy

To my Mother, with love

When it comes to Indian food favourite, the fond thoughts of the tastes of traditional home cooked food comes to fore. The aromas and flavours from mom's kitchen surpass any fine dine experiences. A native of Maharashtra, Roopa Nabar, my mother has penned down a vast array of finger licking recipes, ones which have strong roots in an everyday meal in a typical Marathi home. Her stories which uplift the cooking experience, bringing a native kitchen to life, is a crowning accomplishment.

Personal favourites range from – the western costal specials like Tondli Dabdabit & Spicy Baked Mackerel "Karwari speciality – Bangda Dhodak"; to the Kolhapuri Mutton Rassa. With a unique modern approach on cooking, she has nurtured and developed each dish with brimming authenticity, with use of regional ingredients and most importantly demonstrating usage of traditional tips & techniques in home cooking. She has revived the forgotten methods of cooking festive Indian specialties like the five different ways of making Pohas - a customary part of 'Diwali Faral' and celebrating Rishi Panchami by cooking a pot full of 'Rushi chi Bhaaji' for the family. These recipes hold a vivid and deeply personal connection and go on to create a one-of-a-kind selection.

Proud and privileged to be her son, I am immensely thankful to her for sharing her experiences and her journeys through her kitchen, bringing to us an abundance of flavourful Maharashtrian delicacies to be preserved and cherished.

GAURANG NABAR